The
AFFINITY
PRINCIPLE

PEOPLE FIRST, ALWAYS

A FORMULA FOR
BUSINESS SUCCESS
THROUGH
MINDFUL LEADERSHIP

GRANT IAN GAMBLE

AFFINITYPRINCIPLE.COM

FIRST EDITION

Designed by Jana Gamble, Stella Jackson Creative
stellajacksoncreative.com

ISBN 978-1-7349712-0-0

In loving memory of Emily, and with deepest love and gratitude to my wife Jana and our children, Jack and Ellie.

PEOPLE FIRST,
ALWAYS.™

#peoplefirstalways

#affinityprinciple

@grantiangamble
grantiangamble.com

**Scan this QR code with your phone camera
to follow me on social media!**

#mindfulleadership

Grant Ian Gamble

Grant is a top-rated business growth consultant, author and international speaker. His consulting firm, GIG Consulting, works with clients ranging from global brands to regional startups.

When asked what has underwritten his many successes in the business world, he puts it down to putting people first. Developing leadership teams and growing talented team members leads to great customer experiences. Great customer experiences ensure financial success and sustained growth for companies.

Grant asserts that when there is a strong focus on hiring, acclimating and training team members, companies thrive. The right talent, doing their best work, makes management easy.

Grant has held executive positions with numerous best in category businesses ranging from healthcare to hospitality. From his first blockbuster success at age 23, Grant has championed growth and sustainability through practical and actionable methodologies that he shares with his clients and audiences worldwide.

affiliate • v. /uh-**fil**-i-ay

affiliating, affiliated) o

• n. /uh-**fil**-i-uht/ a person

linked to a larger organiz

– DERIVATIVES **affiliation** n.

– ORIGIN Latin *affiliare* 'adopt a

affinity • n. (pl. **affinities**) 1 a na

liking or understanding between people or thi

relationship between people or thi

with similar qualities. 3 the tendency

chemical substance to combine with

other.

– ORIGIN Latin *affinitas*.

affirm • v. state firmly or publicly.

– DERIVATIVES **affirmation** n.

Latin *affirmare*

-ive • adj.

The
AFFINITY
PRINCIPLE™

This book is designed to help leaders like you attract, retain, and optimize talent. This optimal state arises when your talent is engaged. When your talent is engaged, your customer experience is optimized, your profit follows your customers' experience, and Affinity flows.

---

af·fin·i·ty
noun

1. a natural liking for or attraction to a person, thing, idea, etc.
2. a person, thing, idea, etc., for which such a natural liking or attraction is felt.
3. relationship by marriage or by ties other than those of blood
4. inherent likeness or agreement; close resemblance or connection.

prin·ci·ple
noun

1. a fundamental truth or proposition that serves as the foundation for a system of belief or behavior or for a chain of reasoning.

Talent Makes Capital Dance!

- "Funky Business"

Jonas Ridderstrale & Kjell Nordstrom

CONTENTS

#secretsauce

INTRODUCTION

If you had the means to:

» Improve your customers' reviews and ratings while increasing profitability;

» Decrease absenteeism and improve team member retention;

» Inspire your team members to be the best that they can be;

» Increase productivity and simultaneously reduce defects;

» Grow sales and reduce shrinkage;

» While substantially decreasing safety incidents,

Would you go to the lengths necessary to achieve these outcomes?

What if I suggested that the lengths necessary were not that great and the amount of effort needed was not much more than you already contribute on a daily basis? That achieving these tremendous shifts in momentum is not only realistic, but also incredibly attainable?

My confidence in achieving these outcomes is derived from over 30 years of hands-on experience. It is defined by the mistakes I've made as well as the successes I've achieved. I have seen the Affinity Principle work consistently in both large and small organizations.

These concepts have also been substantiated in studies conducted by a variety of respected academic and research institutions including the Gallup organization that studied over 82,000 teams, more than 1.8 million team members, across 230 organizations, 49 industries, and 73 countries!

So, what's the secret sauce? You could define it as engagement but I am extending the definition to include a natural liking, agreement, and connectedness that expands the concept of engagement into a state of Affinity!

af·fin·i·ty
noun
1. a natural liking for or attraction to a person, thing, idea, etc.
2. a person, thing, idea, etc., for which such a natural liking or attraction is felt.
3. relationship by marriage or by ties other than those of blood
4. inherent likeness or agreement; close resemblance or connection

What Is the Affinity Principle?

"The Affinity Principle" is based on 12 Pillars and Levers of Mindful Leadership, which are the fundamentals of the Affinity Formula.

The premise of the Affinity Formula is simple:

Mindful Leadership creates an incredible Team Performance, which leads to an awesome Customer Experience and that yields great Financial Results.

This book explores the 12 Pillars and Levers of Mindful Leadership and is designed to help leaders attract, retain and optimize talent. "People First, Always" is the mantra of "Affinity," because when your talent is supported, focused, and engaged Affinity thrives.

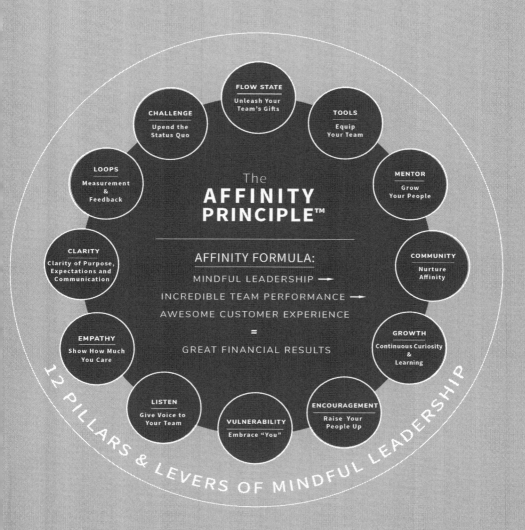

The
AFFINITY PRINCIPLE™

AFFINITY FORMULA:

MINDFUL LEADERSHIP →

INCREDIBLE TEAM PERFORMANCE →

AWESOME CUSTOMER EXPERIENCE

=

GREAT FINANCIAL RESULTS

FLOW STATE
Unleash Your Team's Gifts

CHALLENGE
Upend the Status Quo

TOOLS
Equip Your Team

LOOPS
Measurement & Feedback

MENTOR
Grow Your People

CLARITY
Clarity of Purpose, Expectations and Communication

COMMUNITY
Nurture Affinity

EMPATHY
Show How Much You Care

GROWTH
Continuous Curiosity & Learning

LISTEN
Give Voice to Your Team

VULNERABILITY
Embrace "You"

ENCOURAGEMENT
Raise Your People Up

12 PILLARS & LEVERS OF MINDFUL LEADERSHIP

LEADERSHIP APPRAISAL

Amplify Your Leadership Potential

The Affinity Principle Leadership Appraisal is a free benchmarking tool for you and your leadership team to gauge your individual and collective propensity to create Affinity within your organization.

The tool is based on 54 key questions asked of over 6,000 senior executives across the world in the Globe 2020 Report of CEO Leadership Behaviors and Effectiveness. These 54 questions break down into the following 8 primary leadership categories that most influence top management team's dedication and overall firm performance:

1. Administrative Competence
2. Decisiveness
3. Diplomacy
4. Inspirational
5. Integrity
6. Performance Orientation
7. Team Integration
8. Visionary

Taking this free Leadership Appraisal prior to reading this book may bring some clarity about where to focus your attention. To take the Leadership Appraisal, scan the QR code on the opposite page or go to:

grantiangamble.com/leadership-appraisal-sign-up-form

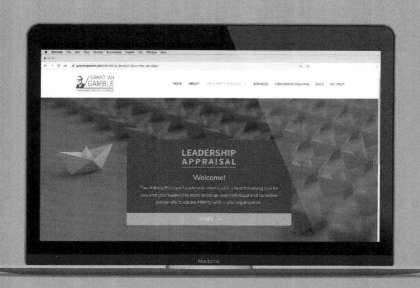

#leadershipappraisal

Once a Boy Scout, Always a Boy Scout

When we have Affinity, we flow.

When we flow, things come easily, stress decreases, focus improves, performance increases, enjoyment, and creativity heighten, and engagement is inevitable.

I have experienced this heightened state many times firsthand, and I always try to create an environment for my team members in which they are able to attain it themselves.

Growing up in Australia, my first raw experiences of this heightened state of team were in the Boy Scouts and later in the Navy. Both of these experiences taught me a lot about leadership and how to engage a team.

Selected from over 5,000 applicants into the Royal Australian Naval College, this exposure to the armed forces cemented many leadership principles and also had me questioning many of the precepts of hierarchy.

This is the day I received my Queen Scout Award. The leaders I was exposed to, and the leadership this experience developed in me, has stayed with me throughout my business career.

#foundations
TRUSTWORTHY
LOYAL
HELPFUL
FRIENDLY
COURTEOUS
KIND

When I joined the Boy Scouts, I was clearly drawn to the broad array of activities such as camping, kayaking, caving, and rock climbing, rather than the more altruistic aspects of service to the community, or the personal and leadership development opportunities the organization offered.

As I became more and more engaged in outdoor activities, these other inherent elements began influencing my intrinsic motivation.

The Queen Scout Award, which is the highest youth award achievable in the Scouting movement in the Commonwealth, focuses a scout on four key areas: Leadership Development, Personal Growth, Community Involvement, and Outdoor Activities.

This award had never been attained by a scout in my district and as I journeyed toward this major achievement, I learned many lessons. In order to receive the Queen Scout Award, I needed to achieve 10 Venturer Level awards and 4 Queen Scout Level awards.

The Queen Scout Award

My Scout Uniform

On this journey, I needed to build trust as well as encourage and inspire my fellow scouts. I actually needed to create Affinity within my scout group to complete a multitude of the requisite endeavors.

Throughout this process, I was constantly exposed to varying degrees of motivation and willingness from my fellow scouts.

I had to learn patience and diplomacy.

As driven as I may have been, I had to accommodate for teammates that did not share my passion for the project at hand.

As I pursued the first tier of the Queen Scout Award, the Venturer Level fell into the following categories; Citizenship, Expeditions, Fitness, Pursuits, Social, Expression, Ideals, Service, Vocations and Environment. Each award held challenges, opportunities, and enlightenment for me as a participant and a leader.

Most of these tasks required me to manage teams in order to achieve a successful outcome.

I then had to expand on four of these areas at the Queen Scout level and I chose Pursuits, Expression, Service and Environment.

As you can see from these broad descriptions, it was a literal smorgasbord of learning, skills, and activities. To give an example of the sorts of things these areas entailed, the Environment award is a pretty compelling example. This was a pursuit I tackled by myself, but it encompassed some tremendous connections and life learnings.

The "Pursuit of the Environment" award actually came out of my passion for paddling. At the age of 14, with Scout Leader Dave's guidance, I built my first fiberglass kayak. In order to get this kayak into the nearest available water, Cockle Creek, I had to make a buggy that I could attach to the back of my bike. I could then ride down to the creek to paddle whenever I had the chance.

As I explored options for the Environment award, our school librarian, Mrs. Dean, introduced me to her husband who worked for what is now the New South Wales Environment Protection Authority. We chatted about the work that he did and the things I was interested in, to see if there was something that might cross over with his area of expertise. We came together on Cockle Creek.

*Cockle Creek, Ku-Ring-Gai Chase
National Park, Australia*

It turns out that one of the biggest factories in the area at the time was suspected of discharging polluted wastewater into the creek that I paddled regularly.

I could personally attest to the number of dead fish and the obvious environmental degradation of the area around the discharge pipes. He explained that the company worked with a lot of heavy metals and other contaminants, but they were regulated in their discharges.

He also explained that he had to announce to the company when he was coming out to test discharges and he suspected what he was testing on his official visits may be very different from what the discharges might normally look like if he were unannounced.

As part of my Environment project, I offered to take regular samples of the discharges into Cockle Creek. We were going to study what fluctuations there were between scheduled tests and my regular samplings and I was going to study the potential impact these discharges might have on the environment.

At regular intervals, I began paddling down to the discharge pipe to take samples. I would supply the samples for testing and over many months built a report on the pollution that was flowing out into this body of water.

This insight into the company's activities showed substantial levels of pollutants well beyond the regulated amounts. My data combined with other data points, such as surveys of airborne contaminants in the local environment, helped strengthen the case for more stringent controls and testing.

This in turn helped reduce waste discharge significantly, but much of the damage was already done.

In 1991, Graeme Batley from the Commonwealth Scientific and Industrial Research Organization said, "Cockle Creek was one of Australia's worst contaminated estuaries and would require dredging to remove high concentrations of lead, zinc and cadmium."

As a young man who had no real idea about industry and its intersection with the environment, or a community, this process was highly enlightening. It exposed me to leadership decisions being made at a corporate level that were not demonstrating conscious capitalism. It exposed me to change agents who wanted to make a difference. It was a rude awakening to the contradictions of risk versus reward.

On the journey to achieving my Queen Scout Award, I learned about community activism, faced physical challenges, constantly had to step outside my comfort zone, and as a result developed character and leadership skills that have served me my entire life.

I was also exposed to passionate leaders and I myself needed to develop and demonstrate leadership as I engaged and activated other scouts around me. Without question, this 5-year journey heightened my sense of working on a team and when I applied to join the Royal Australian Naval College, I believe the Queen Scout Award significantly contributed to my acceptance.

The Royal Australian Naval College

When I was accepted into the Royal Australian Naval College, I was stationed at HMAS Creswell at Jervis Bay, a Naval base three hours south of Sydney, Australia. As it was initially explained to me upon arrival, the primary responsibility of an officer in the Navy was the welfare of their sailors. It was further explained that it was imperative to uphold the Navy's core values of honor, honesty, courage, integrity, and loyalty.

Over the next couple of years, I was exposed to military discipline such as how to wear a uniform with pride, how to conduct myself in an appropriate military manner, and how to interact with other officers as well as sailors. Leadership was also demonstrated to me and spoken about in numerous formal and informal settings.

Probably the biggest change for me was learning to live at close quarters in a communal structure and share heads (toilets) and showers with 20 other cadets. My cabin, uniform and performance were inspected relentlessly and the rhythm of the days started before dawn with a morning run and ocean baths swim and often went past midnight.

Most of all, this grueling schedule focused on teamwork and leadership. The development of mateship with my fellow junior officers was critical in every aspect of my day, ranging from surviving 'shake-ups' in Physical Training through to getting my boat tickets (licenses) which were a pre-requisite to obtaining shore leave.

I believe the indelible lesson that was ingrained into all of us in those couple of years was teamwork.

When we arrived on base, we were a disparate group of young men, full of testosterone and bravado. Very quickly our instructors demonstrated, not so subtly, the need to work seamlessly together.

What at first seemed to be ridiculous routines, requirements and expectations slowly formed into a cohesive system of instilling teamwork and systems into our midst. Everything from the direction our coat hangers faced in our locker through to how our shoelaces were laced had purpose. We were drilled relentlessly, whether it was on the parade ground or working seamlessly together to get the gymnastics equipment out in record time to avoid another punishing shakeup from the Physical Training Instructors.

Throughout this time, our leadership potential was poked and explored through numerous practical exercises where the personal strengths and weaknesses inherent in our team were put to the test. Many lessons in leadership were demonstrated by our senior officers and instructors and in some cases those lessons may have been better termed "contrast correction" (what not to do). This was especially the case with some of the senior cadets, who revelled in abusing their powers and punishing the junior cadets at the least provocation.

In spite of these contrasting styles, I came to learn the benefits of building a cohesive team that faces in the same direction, with clear expectations and a defined intrinsic purpose.

These powerful lessons have helped me create Affinity in teams I've led in some very challenging environments.

Little did I know how much the teamwork and leadership lessons I had learned in the Navy and Boy Scouts, would benefit me in the future.

Flop Socks & Disco Music!

Both the Boy Scouts and the Navy taught me a lot about leadership and how you engage your team. But it wasn't until I bought my first business that I experienced the full effect of Affinity in action. I was 21 years old and had since left the Navy. After trying a bunch of different jobs, I became attracted to the fitness industry. This was the early days of aerobics with spandex, flop socks, and disco music. I loved the energy and enthusiasm of the fitness industry. So much so that I took a massive pay cut (500%) to become a full-time fitness industry worker.

I had undergone my accreditation to teach classes and was teaching 10-20 classes a week. I supplemented my hours by cleaning the locker rooms, vacuuming, working behind the front desk, and supervising the gym floor. The industry didn't pay well, most of the work wasn't very glamorous, but

I LOVED it!

This photo is my teenage kids' worst nightmare. Leading an aerobics competition, in spandex c. 1984

The experience I had at this first fitness center was 'engagement'. I was engaged. That engagement wasn't coming from the management, it was coming from within.

> I was doing work I loved. I was helping people improve their health and their bodies, but most importantly I was help-ing improve their self esteem.
>
> This became the cornerstone of my in-trinsic motivation. I loved helping peo-ple, I loved engaging people, and I loved changing lives.

#purpose

Accidental Businessman

Fast forward to age 23. I was traveling up the East Coast of Australia with my girlfriend in a 4WD camper teaching classes at large and small fitness centers on a road trip around Australia. We arrived in Cairns (North Queensland) and started teaching classes at a club called "Fitness In Motion." Our plan was to top up our bank account and scoot across the top of Australia and head down the West Coast.

We'd been teaching classes, working on the gym floor and selling memberships at Fitness In Motion for about a month and we were planning to head off in a few days. We informed the owners, but they shocked us by telling us that they were closing the doors of the club at the end of the month.

They were going out of business!?!

We were stunned. Collectively we'd sold almost 200 year-long, pre-paid memberships to the club in the previous month. Were all those members going to lose their money?! I didn't understand.

How could they do this to these people? To the team? To us? I felt complicit, because I had been a big part of the membership drive.

The truth was, that this club had closed multiple times at this same location. The gentleman who currently owned the club headed up a large chain of clubs that had gone belly up prior to him landing in Cairns. Was this his MO? Was it orchestrated? Or was it just bad luck? Was the fitness industry model inherently flawed? It was the 80's and clubs were opening and closing all over the place. Or was it poor management? Poor location? Did the team have the right stuff?

Regardless of the reasons, I felt a great deal of responsibility to the members who had recently joined, and those that had been there longer, but would also be out of pocket, without a gym to work out in. Layer on those concerns a fairly healthy mix of naive confidence and you've got a recipe for disaster.

Good intentions backed by great enthusiasm and a complete lack of busi-

#opportunity

ness experience.

The owners made us an offer: we could take on the club, the debts, the leases on the equipment, the lease on the premises, with no immediate foreseeable income (back in those days memberships were all prepaid). All this for a token amount of $10. What a bargain!

There began my journey into business.

At the ripe old age of 23, I had taken on a huge amount of debt in a location that had seen multiple clubs close down. The predominantly part-time team members had been moving awkwardly from club owner to club owner, remaining thankful for their 'day jobs'.

That Sunday night, I gathered the team together and told them of my grand plans for the club. How we were going to work as a team, and drag ourselves from the abyss and build a great club. I described how we were going embrace and welcome each and every member, and we were going to create Affinity! And the rest is history.

The club grew and flourished, the business improved, month on month and before we knew it, we were so busy we had parking problems, with people often having to park blocks away.

We outgrew our premises and started planning for a new club, a bigger club, to take advantage of the momentum that seemed to be growing daily.

So, what changed?

Why was this club with the same location, the same equipment, and the same team members suddenly flourishing?

It had closed its doors, officially and unofficially, four times. The location was the same, the equipment identical, the terms of the lease unchanged. Something had changed, but what was it?

At the time, I likely could not have articulated what the 'secret sauce' was. I might have joked that it was 'brute force and ignorance'. I was opening the club at 6 AM and closing it at 9 PM, then working until midnight developing software that would help manage the club better.
All this energy was not what was driving the momentum behind this club.

What was driving the energy was team . . . Affinity.

Affinity of purpose, collective engagement, focused attention, camaraderie. We'd given people more responsibility with a clear mission and they were excelling.

We had created a 'Why'.

I was employing learnings from the Boy Scouts and the Navy. Where I lacked experience, I was allowing my instincts to guide me.

Importantly, my instincts were anchored by integrity. It was always important to me to do the right thing by everyone, even if it wasn't easy. I engendered trust and encouraged transparency.

The team was more of a steering committee than mere employees. We hung out together, we laughed and cried together, and we became a family. We had a solidarity of purpose, and that purpose was bigger than any single one of us.

I also made plenty of mistakes, but even in spite of all the missteps, we succeeded where others had failed.

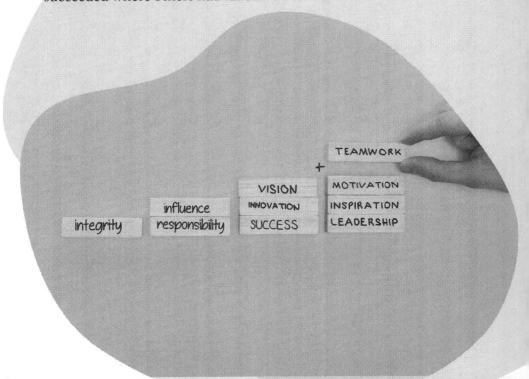

I also led by example.

I taught classes, sold memberships, repaired equipment, built booths for our social club area, and wrote software for our member management system. I was a very hands-on owner and lived and breathed the club along with the team.

This first entrepreneurial experience defined my journey in business.

We went on to sell the club and I used my experience building teams in areas ranging from property development to the hospitality industry. The fitness industry continued to pulse through my veins, and I took on bigger and bigger health & fitness club projects.

Back then, most of the projects I encountered in the fitness industry were resurrection projects. Floundering businesses, large and small, that needed focus and engagement. That needed Affinity to flow through their veins. The fitness industry model was not broken, but lots of good-intentioned operators struggled to create and maintain momentum in their business and their teams.

Each project had its own set of challenges and more often than not I was

SIMPLY PUT, THE AFFINITY PRINCIPLE STARTS WITH YOU: IT STARTS WITH **LEADERSHIP**!

advised, in advance, that I'd most likely need to "restructure the team completely" (code for layoffs and rehiring). And yet as I discovered over, and over again, the team members were rarely the problem. Occasionally there was a troublesome team member, sometimes it was lack of leadership, but most often it was simply letting team members do their best work in a healthy work environment (literally and figuratively).

In the following chapters, I will lay out a very simple formula I have learned and used to create Affinity in all kinds of teams. I have successfully applied these principles directly and indirectly in over 100 companies ranging from small regional businesses, all the way through to national chains.

These tenets are transferable to your business, your department, or your team.
They're scalable and attainable.
Simple and effective.
Proven and implementable.

#leadership

CHAPTER 1

Founded on Leadership

lead·er·ship
noun

1. the action of leading a group of people or an organization.
2. ~~the state or position of being a leader.~~

The definition of leadership is above, but leadership could be further described as "an individual influencing a group of people to achieve a common goal."

That is also an oversimplification, but the most important element of that definition is:

Leadership is dependent on a group or a team to accomplish a goal.

As an effective leader, you can't operate in a vacuum.

And as an *effective* leader, you can't create influence through your title. Great leadership is based on intentional interactions, meaningful relationships, mindful communication, the way you express gratitude and appreciation, your ethics, not your title.

As John Maxwell suggests in his book, *"How Successful People Lead"*

The demands of the leader today make management by position alone "a poor substitute for influence."

In his "21 Irrefutable Laws of Leadership," Maxwell ultimately states, "Leadership ability determines a person's level of effectiveness."

This effectiveness can be attributed to a combination of traits, experience, systems, and training.

It is true that there are some innate qualities that help leaders rise organically, but the vast majority of leadership mojo comes from our innate desire and passion to succeed. This is leveraged when we find fulfillment in what we do by working together with our team.

And the rewards are immense.

Finding that 'sweet spot', defining our purpose, choosing our path, and creating Affinity is not always easy. Regardless of the path we choose and all the technological levers we engage, it is ultimately the channeling of our desire and energy, with the help of other humans, that drives spectacular outcomes.

The greatest achievements of mankind, whether it's reaching out into the Universe or diving deep into the subatomic realm, are achieved by working together.

In the context of traits, I dispute the notion that leaders are born, and not made. I have seen leaders grow under me, above me and around me. The key ingredients are **desire** and **passion**.

#desire

Ultimately, it all comes down to people: people collaborating, engaging, inspiring each other, and working together.

This book explores collaboration, engagement, and Affinity. It outlines a people formula for business that I have successfully employed in over 100 business enterprises I have developed, grown, and rejuvenated throughout my career.

The Affinity Principle is a formula that I have applied successfully in small scale businesses all the way up to large international enterprises. It has withstood the test of time, in different industries, in disparate markets, in spite of economic highs and lows.

As Sun Tzu's "Art of War" clearly demonstrates, there are many factors that affect an outcome in any field of battle (or business), but of all the factors one of the most foundational elements is leadership. The Affinity Principle holds to the same premise.

The "Art of War" is purportedly over 2,500 years old and has strangely morphed from military circles into a best seller in the business world. Its tactics and strategies seem to have withstood the test of time as tenets of war have been transposed into modern business management principles.

It almost defies imagination that in the most disruptive age of business, in the history of mankind, millennium-old principles still hold.

It seems that inevitably, in this world of exponential obsolescence, age-old fundamentals of great leadership will continue to shape the path and trajectory of business.

And the most important by-products of great leadership are team engagement and Affinity.

Whether that's on the battlefield, the sporting field, or in the highly contested realm of business.

Even though leadership, in and of itself, does not guarantee a phenomenal team performance, we do know with certainty that a phenomenal team performance always has a great leader at its focal point.

This gravitational pull that the leader exerts almost certainly translates into outstanding outcomes in that particular field of endeavor.

In the case of business, outstanding outcomes usually relate to the customer experience. Whether the customer is the end consumer, the client, or another business.

Reviews and ultimate transparency are now endemic in business and poor customer experiences will inevitably translate into poor business outcomes.

If we look at this formulaically, it looks something like the following:

So, if all this starts with Mindful Leadership, what does that look like? How do you create it? How does it translate into a great Team Performance? And does this guarantee an Awesome Customer Experience? And importantly, is this formula applicable to all businesses?

This book explores the ultimate applicability of this formula, and most importantly the facets of leadership that drive engagement and ultimately create Affinity.

#applicability

CHAPTER 2

Applicability

ap·pli·ca·bil·i·ty
noun

1. the quality of being relevant or appropriate

In the ever-accelerating race to improve and exceed the achievements of previous generations and iterations of everything, leveraging technology is inevitable.

However, it is our innate agility and creativity as humans that gives us the ability to adapt to this world of augmentation, altered realities, and constant disruption. Provided we're willing to forego the premise of 'business as usual'.

Nowhere is this truer than in the leadership stakes.

As much as it may feel as though humans are moving into the background and technology is moving into the foreground, this need for innate creativity and agility ultimately secures our future as leaders and contributors to growth and success in our organizations.

I also believe we can build on our fundamentals and that the old adage that leaders are born, and not made, is at best flawed.

Science suggests that no more than 30% of leadership traits are innate and 70% is learned and developed.

I think of this in the analogy of sport. I have coached a number of my son's and daughter's soccer teams over the years and have seen young athletes with exceptional athletic abilities excel in the junior leagues. These young boys and girls seemed to have an innate athleticism that they may well have been born with. As they get older the 'natural athletes' that did not continue to work hard on their craft, and nurture their gifts, actually floundered and fell to the wayside. Their innate gifts were not enough.

Conversely, those kids that may not have been as naturally gifted in the early years of their soccer experience oftentimes built their skills and in some cases ended up outperforming the more naturally gifted athletes, through dedication to practice and continued skill development.

My point is that effective leadership may stem from fundamental traits, but those foundational gifts still need to be perfected and refined over time through experience, training and continuing education.

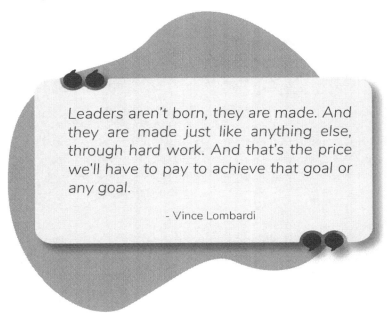

Leaders aren't born, they are made. And they are made just like anything else, through hard work. And that's the price we'll have to pay to achieve that goal or any goal.

- Vince Lombardi

In the GLOBE 2020 CEO Study, 70 researchers collected data from over 1,000 CEOs and over 5,000 senior executives from a variety of industries across 24 countries. Within this study, they determined the primary CEO leadership behaviors that impacted TMT (Top Management Team) Dedication and FCR (Firm Competitive Performance). In ensuing chapters we are going to explore the 8 top behaviors listed on the next page and their relationship in creating Affinity!

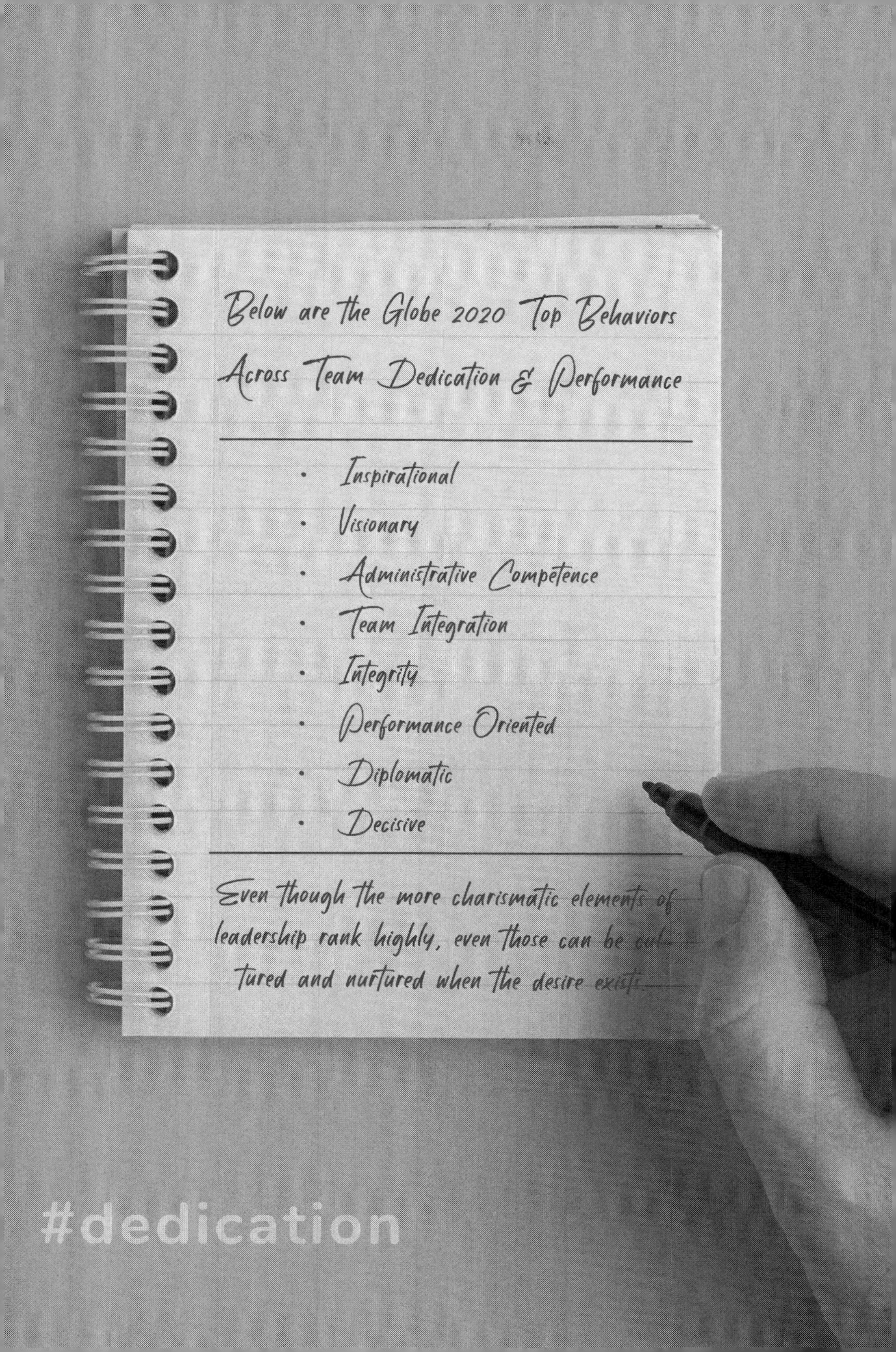

Below are the Globe 2020 Top Behaviors
Across Team Dedication & Performance

- Inspirational
- Visionary
- Administrative Competence
- Team Integration
- Integrity
- Performance Oriented
- Diplomatic
- Decisive

Even though the more charismatic elements of
leadership rank highly, even those can be cul-
tured and nurtured when the desire exists.

#dedication

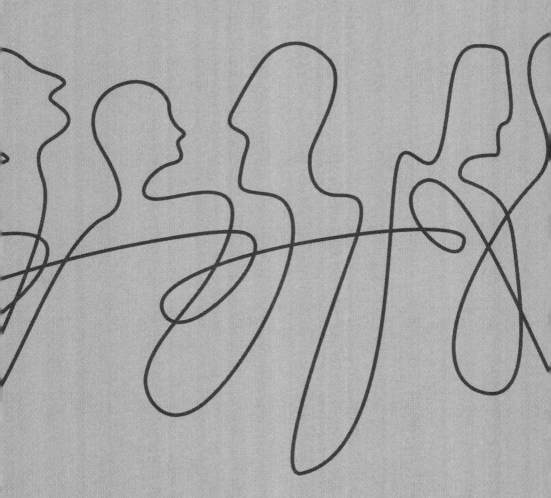

#inspirational

CHAPTER 3

Inspirational - Find Your Center

in·spi·ra·tion·al
adjective

1. providing or showing creative or spiritual inspiration.
    "the team's inspirational captain"

CONNECTEDNESS, HUMILITY, EMPA-
THY, LISTENING SKILLS and VITALITY
are fundamental elements of finding your
center and inspiring others.

As with most attributes, inspiration can come in many shapes and forms. And what inspires one person doesn't always inspire another.

According to recent research conducted over three years by Mark Horwitch and Meredith Whipple Callahan at Bain & Company:

"The most inspiring characteristics of leadership emanate from how you connect with others and include attributes such as humility, empathy, listening skills, and vitality."

The other key point from this study is that you don't need all 33 characteristics detailed in the study to be inspirational. You can have as few as one.

If your one distinguishing strength is in the top 10% of your peer group you're twice as likely to be inspirational.

According to the studies' authors, if you exhibit four or more of these inspirational elements you have over a 90% chance of being more inspirational to your teammates.

What is really heartening is that no particular combination of these elements is statistically more beneficial than another. Inspirational leaders figuratively come in all shapes and sizes.

Obviously, the more strengths you have, the more inspirational you can be and the more likely you are to create Affinity.

And being an inspirational leader brings huge benefits for you and for your team. Being an inspirational leader allows you to connect and motivate your team and the studies' authors also determined that the single

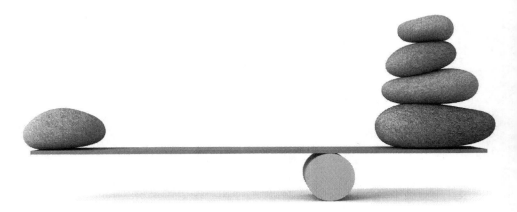

most powerful strength an inspirational leader could have is centeredness. I translate that to mean, being present. We will touch on this throughout this book, as a central theme in creating Affinity.

When we are present in what we're doing, and with the people we are interacting with, we connect on a level that is not replicable with charisma or inspirational overtures.

Authenticity is key! When we are truly and authentically present, we make that individual (or task) the center of the universe.

The Bain and Company researchers suggest that centeredness "improves one's ability to stay level-headed, cope with stress, empathize with others, and listen more deeply." When I have been truly present for my team members, even in the toughest of times, my ability to inspire my team, to maintain Affinity, and navigate those challenging times improved exponentially.

And my goal with any team is to create Affinity. When I am centered and present my ability to read and lead my team is amplified and Affinity thrives.

However, it is easy to get unfocused and distracted when the volume of information and list of priorities continues to increase at an unprecedented rate.

It is incumbent upon the leader to stratify these competing demands and truly be present in those moments that matter.

A classic example of this would be meetings. If you're in a meeting, it is beyond critical that you remain engaged and present. And if you believe that the meeting is not the best use of your time, it is your responsibility to reject the meeting request, or politely step out, versus being in the meeting and not actually being present.

TIP:

Online vs. Off-line Meetings

One key learning I've had over the years is on-line versus off-line. When you see two people spiraling into a one-on-one in a meeting I recommend you suggest they take that conversation off-line, so that everyone else in the room can stay on-line. I recommend that this becomes SOP for your team, and when you have to interject that it is done tactfully. These little course corrections will enhance the value of meetings for all attendees and yourself.

#meetings

By rejecting a meeting request you are stating that your time is more valuable elsewhere, and if the meeting convener feels strongly that they need you in that meeting they need to make that case, or adjust the agenda to better align with what you value as good use of your time.

How many meetings have you been in where there's no formal agenda, laptops are open and people are responding to their emails, phones are in hands and texts are going back and forth (sometimes between people in the meeting) and you're there thinking about all the other things you should be doing?

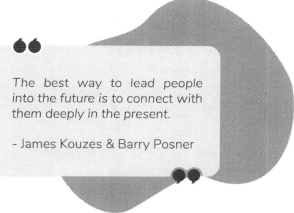

> The best way to lead people into the future is to connect with them deeply in the present.
>
> - James Kouzes & Barry Posner

Whether you realize it or not, your level of distractedness is contributing to the dysfunction of the meeting as much as any of those other poor meeting manners being expressed throughout the room.

When you're engaged and focused, you provide the conduit to focus your team.

If you're present and witnessing this blatant waste of time and resources, you are likely to rein it in. When you are as distracted as many of the other attendees, you don't have the presence of mind to bring the meeting back on point and focus the attention of the attendees on the matters at hand.

Obviously, meetings could be a whole other chapter, but the point of this example is that:

When inspirational leaders bring their focus to the team through their presence they create a level of connectedness or Affinity, that will enhance the impact they have and the alignment and engagement their team feels.

In dysfunctional situations, the mindful leader can reverse the unproductive nature of many rituals people take for granted . . . through their presence.

A key recommendation I have for developing your inspirational assets is to do an audit of the strongest inspirational elements you have in your organization.

Bain & Company have developed a 360-degree assessment based on the views of team members at every level. This input is then cross-tabulated with the individual's peers' results to ascertain his or her relative strength.

Understanding where one's strengths exist helps you define your leadership essence and shape and refine it in your daily interactions.

Focusing on these strengths is far more likely to drive Affinity than trying to rehabilitate your weaknesses.

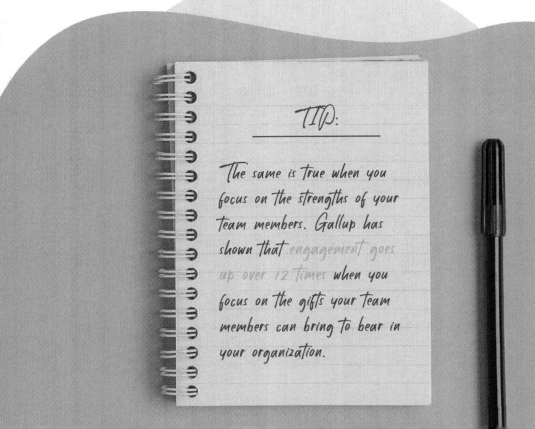

TIP:

The same is true when you focus on the strengths of your team members. Gallup has shown that engagement goes up over 12 times when you focus on the gifts your team members can bring to bear in your organization.

Bain Inspirational Leadership Model

Bain research identified 33 distinct and tangible attributes that are statistically significant in creating inspiration in others. Mark Horwitch and Meredith Whipple Callahan and their research team selected a list of attributes to test based on data gathered from multiple disciplines—including psychology, neurology, sociology, organizational behavior, and management science—as well as extensive interviews.

The result was a set of 33 characteristics that are statistically significant in inspiring others. Bain then used this set of behaviors to create the Bain Inspirational Leadership model (please see page 46). I think it provides an incredible insight into inspiring leadership.

If you review the Leadership Model, you'll see 33 attributes that matter most when inspiring others. Remember that as few as one of these attributes can make you an inspiring leader if you're in the top 10% in that group. And being strong in more than one characteristic almost ensures that you'll be inspirational. Four or more almost guarantees it.

BAIN INSPIRATIONAL LEADERSHIP MODEL

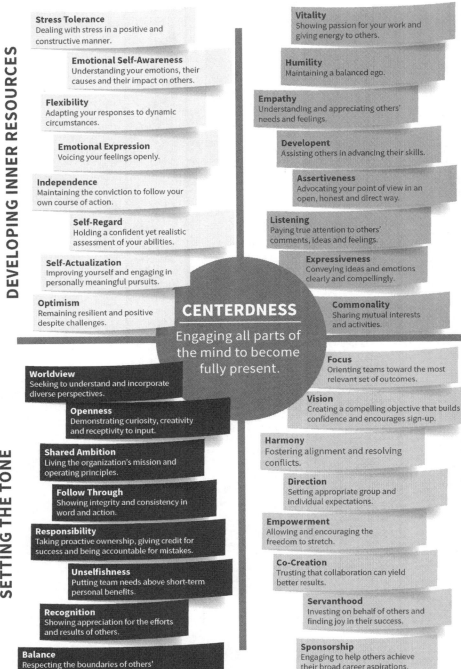

DEVELOPING INNER RESOURCES

Stress Tolerance
Dealing with stress in a positive and constructive manner.

Emotional Self-Awareness
Understanding your emotions, their causes and their impact on others.

Flexibility
Adapting your responses to dynamic circumstances.

Emotional Expression
Voicing your feelings openly.

Independence
Maintaining the conviction to follow your own course of action.

Self-Regard
Holding a confident yet realistic assessment of your abilities.

Self-Actualization
Improving yourself and engaging in personally meaningful pursuits.

Optimism
Remaining resilient and positive despite challenges.

CONNECTING WITH OTHERS

Vitality
Showing passion for your work and giving energy to others.

Humility
Maintaining a balanced ego.

Empathy
Understanding and appreciating others' needs and feelings.

Developent
Assisting others in advancing their skills.

Assertiveness
Advocating your point of view in an open, honest and direct way.

Listening
Paying true attention to others' comments, ideas and feelings.

Expressiveness
Conveying ideas and emotions clearly and compellingly.

Commonality
Sharing mutual interests and activities.

CENTERDNESS
Engaging all parts of the mind to become fully present.

SETTING THE TONE

Worldview
Seeking to understand and incorporate diverse perspectives.

Openness
Demonstrating curiosity, creativity and receptivity to input.

Shared Ambition
Living the organization's mission and operating principles.

Follow Through
Showing integrity and consistency in word and action.

Responsibility
Taking proactive ownership, giving credit for success and being accountable for mistakes.

Unselfishness
Putting team needs above short-term personal benefits.

Recognition
Showing appreciation for the efforts and results of others.

Balance
Respecting the boundaries of others' relationships and commitments outside of work.

LEADING THE TEAM

Focus
Orienting teams toward the most relevant set of outcomes.

Vision
Creating a compelling objective that builds confidence and encourages sign-up.

Harmony
Fostering alignment and resolving conflicts.

Direction
Setting appropriate group and individual expectations.

Empowerment
Allowing and encouraging the freedom to stretch.

Co-Creation
Trusting that collaboration can yield better results.

Servanthood
Investing on behalf of others and finding joy in their success.

Sponsorship
Engaging to help others achieve their broad career aspirations.

Source: Bain & Company

Please remember that all the variables that exist between you and your team ensure that no particular combination of these traits is the 'perfect combination'.

I encourage you to revel in your gifts and focus on those strengths to create the maximum impact you can within your organization, with your stakeholders, and community.

The one trait that I do encourage you to pursue vigorously, even if it is not a strength, is centeredness. For all the reasons I explained earlier, this is the most important attribute.

In the study, centeredness is the most sought after attribute because a state of greater mindfulness will improve your ability to cope with stress, help you keep things in perspective, allow you to empathize with others, and listen more intentionally. All of these abilities will be amplified when you are centered and present and will substantially enhance your ability to lead.

Just as critical as your ability to listen and empathize is humility. The centered leader also has their ego in check. This certainly doesn't mean 'no ego'. Ego is critical to confidence and influence. A balanced ego helps the capable leader trust their judgment and make tough decisions that they think are in the best interests of the team.

Humility is in large measure about walking the walk and talking the talk. It does not mean flaunting your title and privileges; It does mean giving up the dedicated parking space, or the Business Class seat when the team member's you're traveling with are riding back in Coach. It doesn't mean forgetting hierarchy; it does mean trying to flatten your organization.

When the leader flattens their organization by being inclusive and encouraging diversity, and through their actions, magical things happen. When you get down on the floor with your team and jump in when the going gets tough; when you make sacrifices before sacrificing others, you show humility and increase Affinity within your team.

Pope Frances says it really well in the book, "Lead With Humility," by Jeffrey A.Krames.

"Let us never forget that authentic power is service, and that the Pope, (interchangeable with the Leader), too, when exercising power, must enter even more fully into service ."

One of the things I have loved to do for my teams over the years is to host a party for them at my house and cook for them on the barbecue. Or when we have a team lunch at work, I love getting on the grill and cooking for the team. It allows me to do something for them, but I also get to see each one of them as they come through for a burger or a hot dog.

It is essential to remember that the humble and self-effacing servant leader must underwrite their humility with a focus on results.

This includes being inspirational and motivating to your team, and championing change. When layered into the many facets of the strong, centered leader, humility will help create Affinity between you and your team.

The team at Bain and Company also cites vitality as a key element of the inspirational leader.

The energy and vitality that you bring to your company in some ways defines the momentum around you and within the organization. It is a factor in how you inspire and influence your team.

This vitality is underwritten by your passion, optimism and excitement for your people and what you do within the organization.

Vital leaders resonate with their teams and often attract diverse, eclectic, and energetic team members.

Vitality is present in all living things, it is an innate life force, an intrinsic energy. However, maintaining a high level of vitality demands more than the innate energy we all possess. It also needs more than passion itself can fuel. It requires balance and a mindful lifestyle.

Having worked in and around the wellness industry and healthcare for much of my life, I have come to the conclusion that a healthy, balanced, mindful lifestyle can look very different for each person. And key to achieving the vitality that comes with that healthy lifestyle is finding balance.

That means enough exercise to keep your body fluid and energized. Enough good food to fuel that energy. Enough water to keep you hydrated. Enough sleep to rejuvenate you. Enough recreation to recharge you. These are all huge topics that demand a book in and of themselves, but I am sure you have a sense of these fundamental elements.

All of us struggle to find that center that I am advocating. The trick is to keep on trying. The other trick is to be childlike and forgiving in your exploration of these sources of vitality.

The other side of this flow of energy is in your mindfulness practices and that can include meditation, relaxation, breathing methods and stress reduction techniques. Again, maintaining these pursuits can be difficult, but reinforces vitality.

Similarly to the more physical aspects I have mentioned, be childlike and forgiving in your pursuit of balance in this arena as well.

In precis, the mindful leader partakes in activities that will maintain or enhance their vitality.

They challenge themselves constantly and seek balance in their physical and inner awareness.

As the team at Bain and Company outlined in their research, the inspirational leader can have many facets but centeredness is a focal point. I encourage you to seek that mindful place where you accelerate your ability to create Affinity through your energy, presence, and balance.

#visionary

CHAPTER 4

Visionary - Charting a Course

vi·sion·ar·y
adjective

1. Thinking about or planning the future with imagination or wisdom.

Vision and action melded together with inspiration are key ingredients in achieving organizational goals and Affinity.

The visionary leader not only needs to be able to articulate the vision, they also need to be able to focus resources, manage actions (including their own), and marry their passion and sheer will into reality.

The most critical element in transforming a vision into reality is the creation and stewardship of a talented team.

That is the essence of this book.

Leveraged through mindful action, through a talented team, vision can easily transform into reality in the right set of hands.

The visionary leader creates an image of the end goal for their team. That vision often needs to be translated into many forms, for the various constituencies within the business. For the finance team, it may be an inspirational proforma, for the sales team it may be a set of goals laid out to exact the vision, for the production team it may be certain milestones, and so forth.

The visionary leader often needs to chart a course into contested market space and conversely may need to create relevance in uncontested waters, where others may not have ventured. Both these paths become more and more challenging as the market economy continues to expand and diversify.

A key attribute of the visionary is to *see beyond*.

While much of the team is focused on what needs to get done today, this week, this month and this quarter, the visionary is shining the light on the horizon.

This is critical for two reasons:

First, because looking out at the opportunities beyond those that exist today is essential to stay abreast of market forces, let alone ahead of them.

The second compelling need for the visionary within a company is the inspiration that comes from charting a course toward far off places and exotic destinations. My point is that the visionary allows the people that are down on the ground, doing the hard yards, to dream a little and to imagine new things to be achieved and problems to be solved. When you're caught up in the day to day, getting to dream a little along with the leader or founder of the company is a nice respite and can present future opportunities that may not otherwise be apparent.

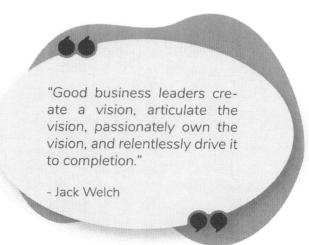

"Good business leaders create a vision, articulate the vision, passionately own the vision, and relentlessly drive it to completion."

- Jack Welch

The vision doesn't always need to be grandiose and should not be so esoteric that many don't subscribe. Sometimes the vision the leader lays out can be around simple things like growing into new premises or new product lines.

From Bullpen to Campus

I was running a company in a small pair of disconnected warehouses and we were popping at the seams. Sales were growing rapidly and the production team was having to get really creative with scheduling and storage. The timing of raw ingredients coming in and production releasing finished product (after Quality Control had signed off) were becoming more and more logistically challenging. We needed new premises but were also a nascent company lacking the financials to underwrite a potential property purchase.

We had been looking for another home for some time and would occasionally mention the search in our weekly All-Team meetings. We had outlined the vision of a campus with outdoor amenities, and room to spare. Easily accessible loading docks, world-class production facilities, nice outdoor seating areas for a sheltered lunch or a brain break.

Our projections suggested this was not only doable but also inevitable if we continued our growth and this vision gave the team something to look forward to themselves. Our search continued and we came across a facility that had been shuttered up for some time but had the bones of the campus we envisioned. Preliminary negotiations with the owner looked promising so we unveiled the vision to the team.

The admin team had been crowded into a bullpen area at the front of one of the warehouses and we were figuratively stacked on top of each other. When they walked around the spacious offices and common areas of this potential new home, even the most pragmatic of them could see past the dust and accumulated junk.

We were able to negotiate a lease to buy and moved in. We subsequently bought this 6-acre campus lock, stock, and barrel and over the course of twelve months, we transformed this deserted warehouse complex into a bustling and energized production, administrative, and shipping facility that allowed the company to take the next leap toward going vertical. We had team events where we carved a trail to a picnic area by the river at the back of the complex so folks could wander in the woods for a bit and get a shaded lunch break away from the hustle and bustle on the other side of the campus.

This was a big vision realized, but the collective energy and Affinity that the team infused into achieving what was needed to bring this vision to life made the realization of this vision all the sweeter.

#mindfulgrowth

CHAPTER 5

Administrative Competence - Maintaining Balance

ad·min·is·tra·tive
adjective

1. relating to the running of a business, organization

com·pe·tence
noun

1. the ability to do something successfully or efficiently

Administrative responsibilities tend to thin out for leaders as they move up the ladder, often morphing from the capacity to do key administrative tasks to the capacity to manage and direct these same tasks and the overall affairs of your organization.

As un-sexy as it seems, administrative competence is cited in GLOBE 2020 as # 3 in the top behaviors across both team dedication and performance.

From my experience, there are critical administrative elements to the consummate leader's influence on the success of their organization.

Successfully running a company, and creating Affinity, typically requires the leader to manage many elements of the business on the way to the top. Competence in managing the disparate and often competing elements of a company requires the leader to be not just capable, but efficient in managing the resources they have at their disposal.

Administrative competence can encompass a plethora of different skills and capabilities ranging from managing the flow and exchange of information for the leaders and their team, all the way through to vetting proformas and balance sheets. It invariably includes managing their time well and ensuring that they prioritize communications and the distribution of resources, including their own time.

Meetings are a classic example where the administrative competence of the leader is demonstrated. Setting meetings, creating agendas, participating in meetings, and not participating in other meetings, are all important skills the leader needs to master.

Seemingly simple things like who gets invited to a meeting can signal an administratively competent leader from one who has been potentially bureaucratized.

If the meeting invite is an egalitarian affair, there are bound to be people in that meeting who could be using their time more productively elsewhere.

I've heard a lot of differing opinions on what a meeting should or shouldn't be, and who should or shouldn't be present. My opinion around meetings is pretty simple: If the meeting is simply a status update unless everyone is updating their status (reference Stand-ups) it shouldn't be a meeting. Send out an email.

A meeting should be a forum for exchange, to teach or train, to solve a problem or brainstorm, and if someone is in the meeting and has nothing to contribute to the dialogue they probably shouldn't be invited.

Meetings should be about an exchange of ideas, or training, they need to be lively and engaging. Opinions need to be tabled, and if there's no discourse there should not be a meeting.

The administratively competent leader should ensure that meetings are productive, engaging and warranted affairs. This begins with the meetings the leader convenes themselves.

Invitations, with an agenda, should ideally be sent out giving all invited participants sufficient time to consider the elements of the agenda and prepare for the meeting.

The meeting should be focused on the topics on the agenda and discourse should stay on track.

The administratively competent leader also creates a space where opinions are respected and trust abounds. In order to get productive dialogue coursing through the meeting, the leader needs to encourage differing opinions and leave white space for those that aren't quick to respond.

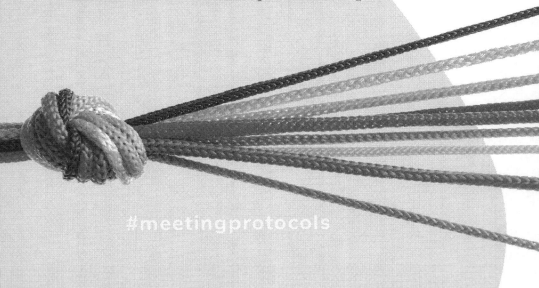

#meetingprotocols

Meetings in and of themselves are an art and a science. They require the leader to ensure adherence to the guidelines set out for the meeting, but equally the leader needs to steward the process and draw the best out of the attendees.

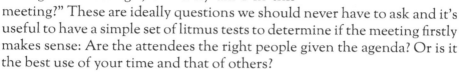

I have to admit that I have attended many meetings where I have asked myself, "Why are we having this meeting?", or "Why am I in this meeting?" These are ideally questions we should never have to ask and it's useful to have a simple set of litmus tests to determine if the meeting firstly makes sense: Are the attendees the right people given the agenda? Or is it the best use of your time and that of others?

There are a huge number of great books written on conducting productive meetings, including everything from "Death by Meetings", by Patrick Lencioni, all the way through to "Meetings Suck", by Cameron Herrold. It feels like the common thread is that most meetings are unproductive and dysfunctional and I believe that underscores the need for leaders to be administratively competent when managing meeting criteria and protocols for their company.

When meetings in your organization are productive and fruitful, they're engaging and challenging, produce results, and bring forth resolutions, the value you exact will far exceed the effort required. Your ability to manage to that outcome is one of the hallmarks of an administratively competent leader.

Meetings are just one example of administrative competence for the leader. Administrative functions and responsibilities range from policies to progress reports, from best practices to benefits, from financial reviews to fiduciary responsibilities. However, I think the message that threads through all elements of your administrative responsibilities is the need from your team to feel like you are managing your resources well, and that includes your time and attention.

NOTE: As companies mature ideally checks and balances go into place, best practices are established, and optimization occurs. But there is a point where administrative oversight and bureaucracy starts to have a negative impact and Affinity diminishes. There is a tenuous relationship between flexibility and control and the administratively gifted leader needs to find that balance at each stage of the business' metamorphosis.

#teamintegration

CHAPTER 6

Team Integration – The Ultimate Advantage

team
noun

1. a group of players forming one side in a competitive game or sport

verb

2. come together as a team to achieve a common goal

in·te·gra·tion
noun

1. the action or process of integrating
2. the intermixing of people or groups previously segregated

The definition of team is both a noun and a verb. And both have applicability in the world of business. Team describes what you have and what you're building. And the verb describes the action of *teaming* up and *teamwork*. Affinity needs to thread through both elements.

Throughout my career, I have made a point of referring to people in the organizations I am involved with as the team and the people on that team as team members. Throughout this book, you won't see references to employees, or staff, but you will see constant references to team members.

To some, this might feel like semantics, but I have witnessed and experienced the difference between being called and treated as an employee and being called and treated as a team member. There is a big difference.

Team "Classic Speed"

At one point in my career, I was running a company that had a manufacturing facility in the Philippines. We were doing nut and bolt rotisserie restorations on classic Mustangs. We essentially took old dilapidated Mustangs, stripped them down to the chassis, and completely rebuilt them to bring them back to their former glory (and beyond).

These cars became much coveted among enthusiasts' circles in Australasia and the company still produces beautiful restomods of this iconic car.

The manufacturing facility was a 100,000 s.f. warehouse located at the old Clark US Air Force base in the Philippines. As I became acclimated to the production facility and the team, I found out that the team members were historically called *workers*. Accepting cultural differences, I still couldn't help referring to the workers as *team members*, and the group as the *team*.

Workers sounded like a benign reference to a bee colony to me. As I watched these gifted tradesmen, and women, ply their respective crafts they looked like anything but worker bees.

When we talked about team members or I referenced the team, I initially got some odd looks, but I think it eventually began to sink in. In order to create these resto-masterpieces, we needed to be a team. We relied on each other for ultimate success, just as a sporting team would.

The team members that were assembled in this company were an amazing, hardworking, and talented group of people and I sensed that being referred to and treated as team members definitely started to have an impact. When you think of yourself as a team member, there is an implicit responsibility to keep up your end of things, because team members are reliant on each other to be successful. They are a part of a whole to which they contribute, and to which they belong.

There had been a few false starts with this company and there were challenges in almost every aspect of the process of bringing these special cars back to life. Little by little, we streamlined, improved and upgraded elements of the process and began to produce cars that were a source of pride and joy to all. Think of it like a small assembly line where the sum total of talent from upholsterers to spray painters produced an amazing result.

There were lots of opportunities to celebrate as a team when cars came off the line and went into the hands of happy customers. Lots of group shots and team members being photographed in front of the cars they had a hand in producing. I imagined that many of those team members were going home and showing off their latest contributions with pride to their families and friends.

Many of the new owners of these classic restomods went on to enter their cars in car shows and would come out with awards in almost every category from upholstery to paint.

From left: A 1966 GT350 Hertz Racer replica; A 1966 Mustang Convertible; A 1965 GT350 Hertz Racer replica

When I left the company, the team bade me farewell and gave me an amazing caricature of me in front of one of the Eleanor Replica's (as seen in the movie "*Gone in 60 Seconds*"). As much as I felt like I had very little to do with the sparkling chrome bumper vehicles that ultimately came out of that facility, I did feel like a part of that team. The amount of appreciation I felt from this team I think reflected the amount of pride I felt being a part of it . . . and maybe that was what we were reflecting off of each other?

Today, that facility continues to produce stunning cars, and I believe that the team members that still make up that organization know that they're a part of a team. I would postulate that a group of workers could not hope to produce the magnificent vehicles this team creates on a regular basis.

When it comes to *team integration*, on one level we build our team to compete against other teams. Yet on another level, we bring a disparate group of people, in a variety of roles, together to complete a series of tasks in unison. And blending dissimilar people together is challenging at the best of times, but incredibly important in building a functional team.

This is part of the inevitable challenge in business, to blend disparate skills, sensibilities, and talents together into a cohesive team = Affinity.

When you can get the right blend of team members working together (often doing very different tasks) with a singular purpose . . . it's magic.

In Patrick Lencioni's "The Five Dysfunctions of Team," Lencioni states, *"Not finance. Not strategy. Not technology. It is teamwork that remains the ultimate competitive advantage."* I believe that holds true today as much as at any time in history.

When team members reference team integration as a key element of what they want from a leader, they are really saying: "I want to be a part of a team," and it is incumbent of the leader to help bring that team together.

A great analogy would be a sporting team. I have coached a lot of soccer teams over the years and learned that I need a mix of talents and dispositions to get a great outcome for the team. I need forwards to drive the ball into the opposition's goal, I need midfielders to defend as well as distribute the ball. The midfielders also help drive the ball toward the opposition's goal. I also need dedicated defenders to protect our goal and get the ball up to the midfielders, and onto the forwards.

My point is that these various players are wired differently, they have different sensibilities. When they're in the right position, it's magic. Conversely, when they're misplaced and operating in a zone that doesn't resonate for them and they aren't comfortable in, they struggle.

Team integration is not only about getting the right players on the field, but it is also equally important to get those right players in their optimal positions.

The last part of team integration is getting them to work seamlessly together. It's tantamount that the different divisions within a company work together. This demands communication and integration. Much like a Venn diagram, there need to be intersections, common elements, and overlap across divisions, in order to bring the company's goals to fruition.

Being a part of a cohesive team is a joy and a fundamental element of optimization.

#integrity

CHAPTER 7

Integrity - Trust & Transparency

in·teg·ri·ty
noun

1. the quality of being honest and having strong moral principles; moral uprightness

2. the state of being whole and undivided

I think back on my experiences in the Boy Scouts and the Navy, and times since. I review the leaders I have been drawn to, and those that I have been repelled by, over the years. One truism holds in all cases: I struggle to follow a leader without integrity.

As it relates to business, Part 2 of the definition above really sums up the impact of integrity for me. Without integrity in leadership, division and fragmentation are inevitable.

The leader who does not *consistently* exhibit integrity in their words, and actions, will ultimately undermine trust within their organization.

Without trust in your organization, most aspects that define a functional team disappear.

"The supreme quality for leadership is unquestionably integrity. Without it, no real success is possible, no matter whether it is on a section gang, a football field, in an army, or in an office." - Dwight D. Eisenhower

Integrity is critical a critical element of Affinity.

I also contend that the integrity exhibited by the leader of an organization directly affects the happiness of their team.

In the World Happiness Report 2016, the research team found that lack of social trust significantly undermined a country's happiness scores. This applies to the microcosm of business equally as much.

It is paradoxical to think that a team can be functional, and in turn be happy, where trust and integrity do not exist.

Nowhere does this affect an organization more than in the ability to be transparent.

In order for team members to have trust, they need to have an Affinity with and for the leader and the organization.

When the integrity of the leader is in question, the ability to have open dialogue and be transparent is typically undermined.

> The best managers promote open dialogue and provide honest feedback on employees' opinions and ideas.
>
> -Gallup's "Building a High-Development Culture Through Your Employees Engagement Strategy" Report

And trust in the leaders, or managers, of an organization, will be reinforced through this open dialogue and transparency. Trust that they will listen openly, that they will appreciate the team members' motivation (assuming the motivation comes from a good place) and will give honest feedback.

And trust needs to flow both ways.

It is rarely the tough words of a truthful leader that hurt, but often the platitudes of a disingenuous leader that ultimately create the most damage.

I sat in the C-Suite of a large organization for several years and we recruited a new C-Suite team member to shore up our executive group. On face value, they appeared to be an affable, friendly, and high integrity individual. What became obvious over time was this individual's inability to trust people. Their inherent distrust ended up being mirrored back from the organization and cultural integrity slowly eroded around that person.

When trust flows down, it will also flow up, but I contend that the trust continuum needs to start at the top.

And if trust is the foundation for all positive human interactions, and relationships, we need to understand the components of trust.

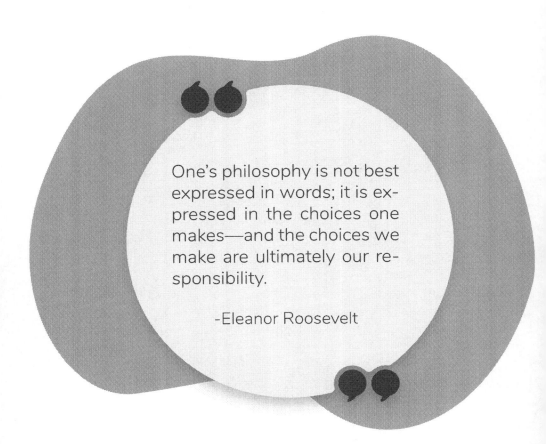

One's philosophy is not best expressed in words; it is expressed in the choices one makes—and the choices we make are ultimately our responsibility.

-Eleanor Roosevelt

Frances Frei's Triangle of Trust

According to Frances Frei, a professor of technology and operations management at Harvard Business School, there's a triangle of trust. The points on that triangle are Authenticity, Logic (rigor), and Empathy . . . this resonates!

I don't just like Frei's definition, I love it! I love it because it resonates so strongly with my experience in companies where trust and integrity served as pillars and equally it highlights the missing elements in companies where trust was scarce.

When a company seeks to create Affinity, Authenticity, Logic and Empathy must be the center points.

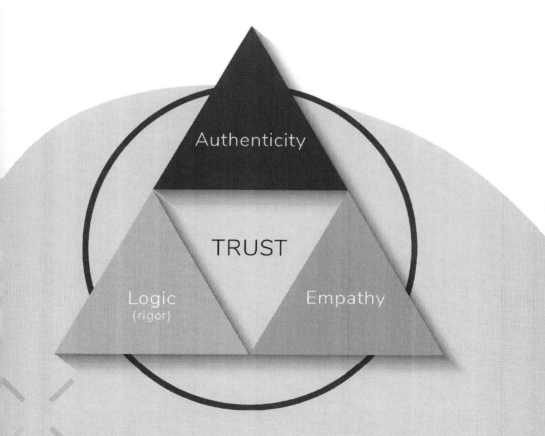

• Triangle of Trust: Authenticity

The tip of Frei's Triangle of Trust is authenticity.

Authenticity firstly demands that we are true to ourselves and in turn present our true selves, unapologetically, to our fellow team members.

Being authentic removes the facade that inevitably crumbles at the worst of times. When things get tough, maintaining a facade often becomes untenable. In challenging times we need to know who it is we're depending on in our team, including ourselves. Where authenticity is present in abundance Affinity abounds.

When we present our authentic self, our team is invited to present their own authentic self. Very often there are parts of ourselves we'd love to keep hidden, but being at the pointy end of a company inadvertently puts us under the microscope, so being anything other than authentic will ultimately lead to distrust and our integrity will slide too.

From very early on, most of us have developed skins to help us fit in. Over time, these skins can become somewhat intractable. But for the leader who wants to create Affinity there can be no more powerful lever than to be your authentic self . . . to be real, not perfect.

Be Real, not Perfect

When we've spent much of our lives diligently crafting an illusion it becomes difficult to distinguish where the skin begins and the real self exists. But fear often prevents us from lifting the veil.

What happens when we're our authentic self is that we are going to not resonate with some people, we're not going to fit in everywhere, not everyone is going to like us. But let's face it: how does that change anything? While we're doing the dance, and not being our authentic self, people who might be attracted to our real self may be having the same reaction you're trying to avoid with the constituency you're trying to win over by pretending.

Truth be told, it takes a lot less energy, and is a whole lot less stressful to be yourself. If you're consistently yourself even the team members that may not like the real you will grow in Affinity.

They at least see you as authentic. And in most cases, those same team members would more likely prefer someone authentic to someone they see constantly morphing for the audience.

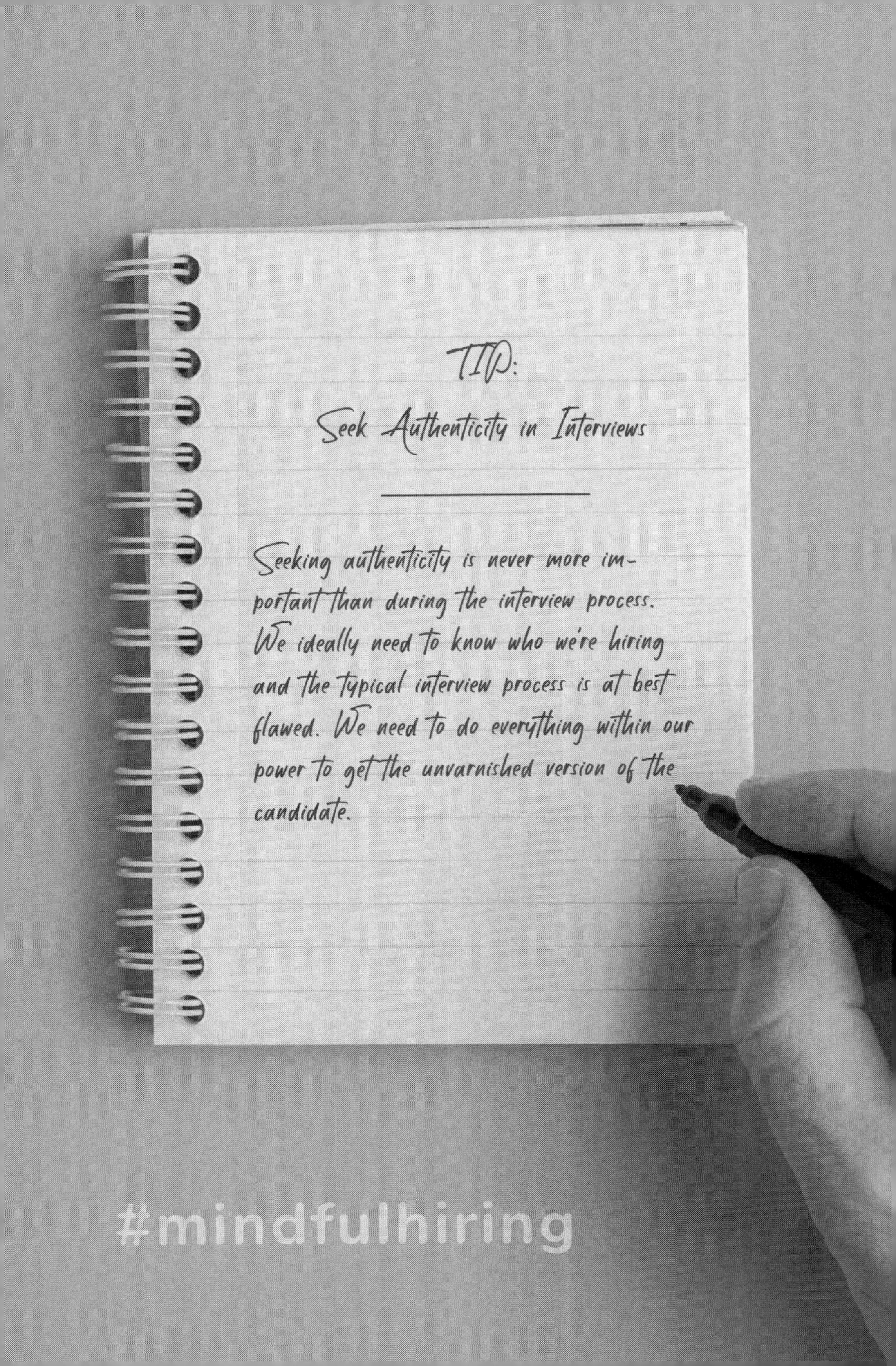

TIP:

Seek Authenticity in Interviews

Seeking authenticity is never more important than during the interview process. We ideally need to know who we're hiring and the typical interview process is at best flawed. We need to do everything within our power to get the unvarnished version of the candidate.

#mindfulhiring

A very successful business mentor of mine hired a lot of family members, and people he knew. This comes with its obvious complications but he preferred to hire people where he had a window into what they were like on their best day, as well as their worst day. This reduced the risk of the interviewee putting on a good show. The old adage, *Better the Devil you know than the Devil you don't*, can be a great truism.

When you have an authentic view of a candidate you can much more easily determine if there will be an Affinity for the job, the team, and your company.

THOUGHT: *Isn't this best for the candidate as well? If they're busy trying to be something they're not it becomes harder and harder to maintain this facade. Ultimately the happiness they felt in securing the job wanes as the pressure to be other than themselves takes its toll.*

Authenticity is hard to uncover in the course of a few interviews though, without additional input. So, getting as many data points and references over time helps. In fact, seeing people *over time* is immensely illuminating.

One technique I have used successfully is the *steeplechase*. Essentially, we would create a series of hurdles that each applicant needed to navigate. The individual would go through multiple interviews, organic checks and balances, with a variety of different people and layers of the organization.

This usually takes weeks and the layers beneath would begin to appear as sometimes their motivation waned, or their facade unraveled.

This was not meant to frustrate a candidate, but it was meant to test them. As we would get a stronger sense of the candidate, they in turn got more and more of a sense of who our company was and what it represented. Some candidates would self-select out, realizing they weren't a good fit or that they didn't have enough of a desire to jump through the hoops we placed in front of them. As a result, we tended to attract resilient, motivated and aligned team members and the pain, and sometimes unintended attrition, of this rigorous hiring process was well worthwhile.

These hurdles would extend to group interviews, especially for customer-facing candidates. It's great to see how the candidate manages themselves in this environment, and how they treat the other candidates. Having the candidate shadow for their position is also a great tool. and watching the candidate when they don't think you're watching can be incredibly telling. Ideally, you catch them exceeding your expectations, but sometimes you see elements of their behavior they'd rather you didn't know about.

I also ask interviewers to check in with other team members the candidate has interfaced with, often by chance. It's very telling to find out how the candidate treated them. It is especially important to get insights from the people that seem likely to have the least to do with the ultimate decision to hire. It's amazing how often the candidate has been rude to a receptionist, or one of the cleaning team, thinking that they wouldn't affect their chances of getting the job.

If we became aware of a candidate treating a team member with anything but courtesy, they became an immediate 'no go'. If they weren't going to be respectful to a team member during an interview process, you don't want to find out how rude they'd be when they weren't supposedly on their best behavior. Especially if they would ultimately be managing some of those team members.

Essentially, we make it a somewhat arduous process to get a position with the company, because we really want people who are motivated, tenacious and want the job badly enough to jump a lot of hurdles to get to the final cut. Ultimately, we want as an authentic view of the candidate as possible and if we push a few over the edge on the way it's worth it to get those resilient and resolute individuals that will be by your side in the tough times.

Hiring is a critical place to look for authenticity but your ability to be authentic as a leader, and to ultimately create Affinity, will always set the tone for your existing and new team members.

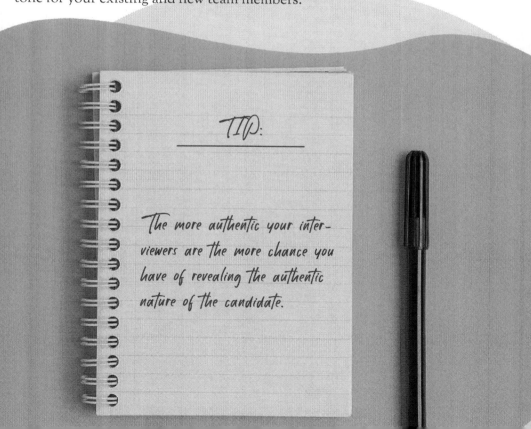

TIP:

The more authentic your interviewers are the more chance you have of revealing the authentic nature of the candidate.

• Triangle of Trust: Logic

The second point on Frei's Triangle of Trust is Logic. I find this component to be another substantial element of establishing trust and Affinity within your team. The very quality of an individual's logic can tell you an enormous amount about them as an individual. Equally, being able to convey that logic succinctly and accurately is tantamount to a leader.

Frei suggests that when you're trying to make a point, open with the essence of your point and expand on it as needed.

In other circles, this might be called your elevator pitch. Frei points out that sometimes what we're trying to present gets lost in the monologue or worse still, derailed in the course of dialogue. At least when you present your point in your opening statement, you've put the substance of your logic front and center.

I have worked with many incredibly smart people over the years and a few of those people have been very good at talking, but one particular leader I worked with became estranged from their team because they would monologue literally for hours and if there was a point in all of the verbosity, it was often lost. That same leader lost traction with the majority of the team over time because they spent so much time trying to prove how smart they were, most team members checked out in advance of hearing the punchline.

• Triangle of Trust: Empathy

The last tip of Frei's Triangle of Trust is Empathy. I feel at its essence this is *presence*, but it is more than that.

Essential to empathy is the need to be completely in the moment with the individual. Equally critical in that moment is the ability to try and put yourself in that person's shoes.

To feel into what they're conveying. When we're present, this is much easier and when we're not present, trying to be genuinely empathetic or create Affinity is impossible.

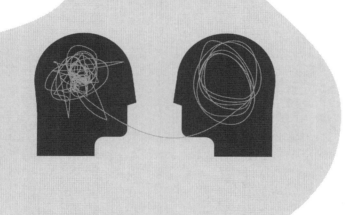

When we focus on the person who needs our empathy and we avoid distractions, we are far more likely to resonate with them and display true empathy for them and their situation.

And how we get *in the moment* with that person depends on the situation.

If you are on a call with a person that needs your empathy, I actually recommend closing your eyes and focusing on the content and nuance of tone as much as possible. This helps you avoid visual distractions, like email pop-ups, and allows you to focus your attention on your auditory input. This will help narrow the gap between the two of you and help you be present, from afar.

When we're face to face with someone, we have the additional advantage of visual input. This is a very powerful element and much of what we see is seen through the subconscious. However, it is important to avoid other distracting visual stimuli like a cell phone or a computer and focus on the person in front of you.

When you look into a person's eyes, a powerful connection is created, and empathy is enhanced.

Empathizing in an email or text exchange seems to be the most difficult way to truly connect, especially in stressful situations. A good rule of thumb for me is to read the text or email at least twice before considering replying. It's amazing what we miss in the first pass.

I also recommend trying to understand the underlying motivation of the writer in order to put more context and texture to the exchange.

I also suggest re-reading the person's piece one more time, after writing your response, and in turn re-reading your response before resending. All this seems rather onerous, but a lot of challenging email and text exchanges I've had have definitely not ticked the empathy box, upon review. I have often been quick to offer solutions and slow to provide empathy. Very often people simply need you to relate, and not resolve.

NOTE: This set of suggestions is meant for exchanges that need empathy, and not simply the stuff of everyday emails and texts.

The more basic need for team members, family, and friends is to be heard and understood and I have come to realize that . . .

empathy is a far more powerful salve than a solution.

For fear of repeating myself I will reiterate that when we are fully present with someone, listening intently, allowing our senses to fully absorb the nuance in the communication, our emotional intelligence (EQ) goes up, our ability to relate to the individual is heightened, and Affinity abounds.

When we display genuine empathy, we reap benefits that a solution could only partially provide.

Ultimately, what we're creating is trust, and in that regard, empathy is a *non-negotiable*.

Frei's overarching premise is that if you have all three elements: Authenticity, Logic and Empathy, and you display them consistently, you will hold a place of integrity and trust in your team's heart . . . And I hold that Affinity will flourish.

#performanceoriented

CHAPTER 8

Performance Oriented - Focusing Energy

per·for·mance
noun

1. An action, task, or operation, seen in terms of how successfully it was performed

o·ri·ented
verb past participative

1. guide (someone) physically in a specified direction

2. adjust or tailor (something) to specified circumstances or needs

The GLOBE 2020 Report found that the dedication and performance of teams was enhanced by a leader's *performance orientation*. This behavior also helps drive Affinity.

One thing that courses through most teams' veins is the desire to win. To be part of something special.

And the performance orientation of their leader is a key attribute in dedicated and high performance teams that achieve Affinity.

As the definitions suggest, the leader helps guide their team toward successfully performing their tasks, which leads to improved outcomes.

I love the analogy of the guide helping people find their way, and as with all guides, it's ideal not to leave anyone behind. This is where shared and well-articulated goals and encouragement can lead teams to significant performance improvements.

As I have suggested in prior illustrations, what works to inspire one team member may not work to inspire another. The performance-oriented leader needs to find the resonant frequency the company, teams, and individuals need in order to focus their energy on the performance outcomes needed. This demands that the performance oriented leader knows their people and their teams on as many levels as possible.

In striving for Affinity, the performance-oriented leader needs to be many things. A guide, a coach, a mentor, a gatekeeper and a taskmaster. You need to ensure that what's being measured are the elements that will result in the performance improvements you and your company are seeking.

The bottom line is that a performance-oriented culture is again going to be founded on trust. In a high-performance company, responsibility and accountability are critical. These elements are underwritten by trust. The successful performance-oriented leader provides clear expectations and consistently applies focus to those goals.

#diplomatic

CHAPTER 9

Diplomatic - Fostering Collaboration

dip·lo·mat·ic
adjective

1. of or concerning the profession, activity, or skill of managing relations.

dip·lo·mat
noun

1. a person who can deal with people in a sensitive and effective way

The consummate leader needs to be both a diplomat and a truth-teller, and those things don't always line up perfectly.

It is the role of the leader to guide their company and oftentimes that involves smoothing the waters and sometimes delivering bad news.

The skills of the diplomat are those of sensitivity toward the stakeholders and finding a navigable path when things get bent out of shape. The diplomat needs to balance often disparate needs to find a resolution.

The diplomat is also the *integrator* who attempts to get everyone playing together in the sandbox and help engender cooperation and collaboration.

As much as dedicated and high performing teams cite diplomacy as a preferred behavior for their leaders, the diplomatic approach comes with some challenges. As I suggested earlier, it can cause the leader to hold back on delivering *truth bombs* when candor may potentially lead to a better ultimate outcome. These compromises can blur the lines at times.

The other downside of the diplomatic style is that oftentimes, taking a more diplomatic route can increase time to resolution. This is usually the case because the diplomatic leader needs to work with all stakeholders. Taking the time to reach out to, and often revisit, all the players doesn't usually happen quickly, but can help amplify Affinity.

I personally think the diplomatic style can be incredibly important in organizations seeking integration and collaboration. It's not always the best style in start-ups, early-stage, and fast-moving organizations though.

Ichak Adizes places great importance on the integrator, or diplomat, and sees them as critical to a company's drive to *prime* (optimal performance).

The Adizes Model

Adizes developed a model of the life-cycle of a business and profiles the different styles of leadership needed at each phase of a company's evolution.

Adizes argues that there are four basic roles that are needed in all organizations, in varying degrees, at various points in a company's evolution: Producer (P), Administrator (A), Entrepreneur (E), and Integrator (I).

People don't fit exactly into one of these, but usually are a mixture of them.

▶▶ The Producer: Organizations exist to produce results. The results being produced may vary depending on the organization, but they all exist in order to satisfy customer needs. The Producer is typically very delivery focused. They work long hours to 'do it now' and tend to believe that hard work solves everything.

▶▶ The Administrator: While the Producer focuses on what to do, the administrator focuses on how things should be done. The administrator undertakes activities that are directed at getting things organized, planned, scheduled, systematized, and generally under control by capturing the learning curve about how to do things right in processes, procedures, and systems.

▶▶ The Entrepreneur: Entrepreneurs embrace change and inspire those around them. They are focused on creating new opportunities or responding to threats. Entrepreneurs are more willing to believe in visions and take significant risks, whilst using story-telling and other techniques to bring others along with them.

▶▶ The Integrator: Integrators are reliable, trustworthy, warm, and caring. The Integrator role focuses on the development of teams who can make the organization efficient over the long term. Integrator Managers often develop persistent cultures of mutual trust and mutual respect.

Source adizes.com

The model below illustrates the varied emphasis needed from these roles as the company matures and ages.

To me, the diplomat is the Integrator.

As you can see in the model illustrated below, the 'I' comes into their own, focusing on cooperation and collaboration of the team as the company matures and the fast-paced chaos of the early stages disappears into the rearview mirror.

I have served as the Integrator in many roles, helping at times manage interpersonal, interdepartmental, supplier and customer relationships. All of these roles require diplomatic skills.

An integrator can be thought of as a Chief of Staff. They aim to foster improved communications up and down the organization and create Affinity. Much like a diplomat they need to be aware and responsive to the needs, views, motivations and conflicts at play.

The integrator considers all the stakeholders and tries to align interests and concerns.

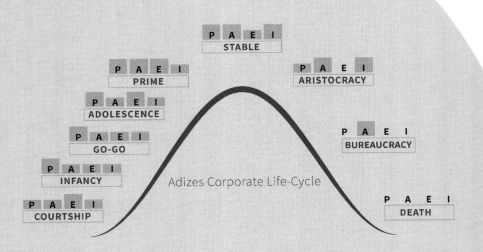

Adapted from adizes.com/lifecycle

The integrator aims for collaboration, cohesiveness and unification.

It is also the job of the integrator to help build teams, and drive toward the shared vision and intrinsic purpose.

And the integrator is uniquely aware of the interpersonal and group interactions and dynamics and works to build the organic functionality of the organization.

#decisive

CHAPTER 10

Decisive - Timely & Thoughtful

de·ci·sive
adjective

1. Settling an issue; producing a definite result

2. (of a person) having or showing the ability to make decisions quickly and effectively

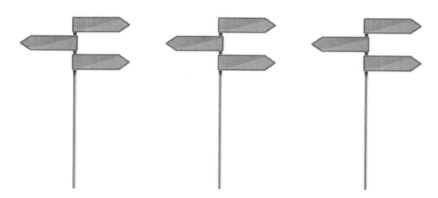

This is the final behavior highlighted in the GLOBE 2020 CEO Study. Just to reiterate, the basis of this study was data from over 1,000 CEO's and over 5,000 senior executives from a variety of industries across 24 countries. The study determined the primary CEO leadership behaviors that impacted TMT (Top Management Team) Dedication and FCR (Firm Competitive Performance).

The ability to be decisive often defines a leader. Equally the ability to make timely and thoughtful decisions will enhance the team's trust and ultimately the Affinity within the team.

A leader who struggles to make decisions, or vacillates often, can lose the confidence of a team very quickly.

Decisiveness is a hallmark of a leader and teams want a decisive leader. The leader who acts with decisiveness invokes confidence. The quality of those decisions will be a factor over time, but inaction and the inability to make a decision when there's sufficient information to justify it, can be the hubris of any company in growth mode.

It also needs to be acknowledged that occasionally you will make a poor decision.

I believe it is a given that the leader who acknowledges a poor decision, when it occurs, will engender and reinforce trust. Most people will accept the occasional misstep unless poor decision making is the norm

Jack Welch argues that a leader can't always wait for all of the desired data points and information to make a fully informed decision. He argues if you wait until you have 100% certainty about a decision the competition will eat you up. The quote below underlines this point.

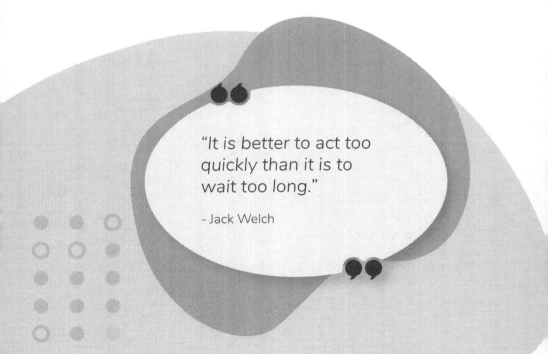

"It is better to act too quickly than it is to wait too long."

- Jack Welch

If you feel you struggle in this area surround yourself with talent and leverage that collective expertise to help increase your confidence around making important decisions. When you have smart, independent thinkers with Affinity, and you listen to their opinions, your decision making will reflect this depth and breadth of influences.

Data is a crucial ally to good decision making and as companies mature and data accumulates, provided you can focus the lens on the data that is useful, you will continue to improve your decision making.

The hard part is the unknown factors, the curveballs. This is where art blends with science in the responsibilities of the leader.

When markets change, consumer behavior takes a turn, or some significant event derails your best-laid plans, this is when the leader needs to draw on their experience, and the collective experience of the team.

Amazon: The Wild West

A good example of a challenging space to be making decisions in is Amazon. I was running a company that made products that we sold through a number of channels, one of which was Amazon. We would regularly lose the "Buy Box" (a feature on Amazon through which the seller achieves much higher sales) and occasionally we'd have a product taken down for no apparent reason. Most of the time we were making tough decisions with very limited information and potentially significant consequences.

The Amazon algorithm is much like the Google algorithm, a moving target, or maybe more aptly a *black box*. The Amazon algorithm is constantly being modified and adapted based on a myriad of different factors and forces.

We would hire the best experts, draw on veteran Amazon users, and pore over our data to try and work out what was going on with this ever-changing set of rules. To be honest, it often felt like there was no rhyme or reason to decisions on their end, and that made decisions on our end even tougher.

And the experts would be as perplexed as we were.

We quickly realized that this juggernaut was like the Wild West: unruly, disorganized, demanding decisiveness, and yet fraught with peril.

We also realized that we needed to be both attentive and resilient: it would take a great deal of focus to excel in this marketplace.

On a regular basis, we needed to make decisions that were more founded on instincts than any data because the data we had was apparently irrelevant. The team member who managed Amazon was amazing. We had hired her to learn Amazon from the ground up. Her background was in programming and she was incredibly resilient, detail-oriented, and tenacious. We needed all of those attributes to battle with "Goliath" on what seemed like a daily basis.

We would routinely convene impromptu think tanks to discuss the latest twist Amazon had thrown at us and ultimately the buck would stop with me. I made a lot of decisions based on the experts' advice and the latest thinking on the Amazon conundrum, our team members' input, and gut instincts. A lot of those decisions panned out, but a number did not.

One of the biggest decisions we made was to pull all independent distributors off Amazon.

This was contentious because we had good distributors selling a lot of product, but there were also many illegal sellers who would grab the buy box by cutting their price and our distributors felt compelled to chase them down that rabbit hole.

Between the legitimate sellers and the unapproved sellers, the discounting heavily impacted our company's Amazon performance. It was truly the *Wild West*. This demanded some tough decisions to be made and ultimately given all the factors at play, we made a monumental, and risky decision to pull all independent distributors off Amazon and heavily police rogue sellers.

The sum total of this decision and all the associated decisions helped us climb up the Amazon ladder and we went from approximately $30k per month to $750k per month in sales in less than 18 months.

This pushed the Amazon channel to around 40% of our total gross income, for that line of products. This in turn demanded a whole new set of decisions to be made around this platform.

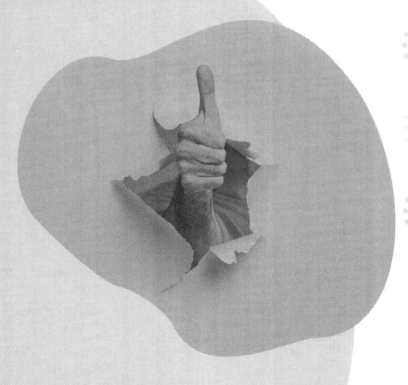

This is a great example of decision making when you don't have all the information, data is scarce, and there is an enormous amount of unknowns. The sum total of decisions on advertising, fulfillment options, absorbing costs to maintain volume, pushing the envelope with Amazon (what we could and couldn't do) was incredibly tough in such a nebulous space. Add to that playing Whack-a-Mole with rogue sellers in the market, who constantly popped up illegally selling our products and drove a whole *other* set of policing and enforcing decision making challenges.

And there were times when we made bold decisions and they paid off, and there were times when a decision would blow up in our face.

My point is that if we had hunkered down and waited for things to settle down, or to have all the information in hand to make a perfect decision, we'd still be waiting and getting *nickeled and dimed*.

Then came the next set of decisions: do we keep the pedal on the gas, or do we let the other channels catch up? There were two key reasons for even questioning this:

First is the fact that Amazon owns the customer. Amazon puts up walls to protect their customers when in actual fact it is a shared customer. So, for every new customer on Amazon, we'd have almost no means to nurture or leverage that customer, to seek referrals or get other products into their hands without triggering Amazon's ire.

So, we now had to decide whether to keep pushing this channel or put our efforts into expanding the channels where we *owned* the customer.

This was debated long and hard, but one decision stayed constant: we needed to ensure that our other channels, where the customer was ours, were being nurtured to their full potential.

It was tempting to throw everything behind Amazon given its trajectory, but the potential of becoming dependent on such a volatile partner was sobering.

That was the second reason for questioning a full-throttle approach to Amazon. The simple fact that Amazon would pull a product off at any time with little to no reasonable justification. This was maddening. What's more, unlike a retail partner that you can have a conversation with, getting to talk to a person at Amazon, who actually has the ability to do anything about the unwieldy monster, was almost impossible. The fact that 40% of our income could dry up instantly, for an undetermined period of time, put us at a huge risk. Imagine if this was 70% to 80% of our income!

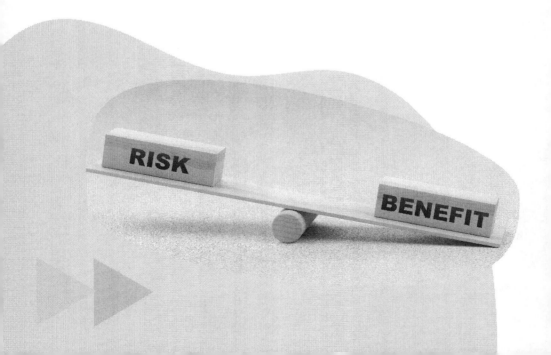

We decided to grow Amazon judiciously and to try to balance this growth against the other channels we were nurturing. We had to make decisions around making our fulfillment equal or better than that of Amazon's and attracting customers to non-Amazon channels versus Amazon.

Pricing was a huge piece of this puzzle. We locked our pricing on Amazon and restricted our vendors' pricing on-line. This was another tough decision that paid dividends and a tough move in this highly competitive online space.

I use this example because I feel that our decision-making skills and instincts were really put to the test almost on a daily basis. The contributions I received from everyone from the experts to our homegrown Amazon champion were invaluable in making final strategic decisions in this volatile space.

I also appreciated the debates and heated discussions we would have at an executive and strategic level. Without the Affinity that flowed in that company, those healthy debates would never have happened.

All these factors helped shape our collective decision making and challenged me as a leader. I am sure the debate goes on today, but I personally feel really good about the decisions made because they were not made in isolation. Even amid all the stops and starts, we kept the momentum pointed in the right direction by being decisive.

CHAPTER 11

Clarity - Purpose and Expectations

Providing and communicating a clear purpose and a consistent set of expectations for team members is not as ubiquitous in business today as you might think.

In early-stage startups, chaos usually reigns. As structure forms and the team grows, plans change, and strategy shifts. The rubber's hitting the road, stress is usually high, and clarity (and Affinity) is rare.

Even as companies mature clarity of purpose and expectations often becomes more clouded.

As clear as the strategy may be in your head, oftentimes team members feel ill-informed and unsure of exactly what they should be doing.

I consult with a wide range of companies from the beverage industry to hospitality, and when I spend time with team members and management teams, lack of clarity and poor communications are consistent, and persistent issues.

If you feel your organization lacks clarity of purpose or expectations, I encourage you to start with the 'why'.

When we seek Affinity for our team, they need context to drive motivation, and the 'why' provides a much deeper connection than the 'What'. They need a meaningful common goal that morphs them from a group of individuals each doing a job (potentially in isolation) into a team with a purpose with clear expectations of them and the ideal outcome of their efforts.

The 'why' of your company needs to be compelling.

For a long time, this 'why' has been termed the 'mission statement'. In recent years, I have come to think of it more as your intrinsic purpose.

That's Nice, But Can You Be More Specific?

I came on-board at a company that had huge aspirations to change the world. These aspirations were certainly inspiring, but equally ill-defined. It was evident that the company was populated with a lot of incredible people, but its lack of clarity of purpose and expectations was telling.

We started having discussions in our weekly All-Team meetings. These discussions swirled around our overarching purpose and values. As we began to hone-in on some central themes and a few nuggets appeared in these conversations, we convened a Strategic Planning Retreat.

The goal of the retreat was primarily to better define our intrinsic purpose and our core values.

Defining and communicating the 'why' is a process which takes time. Any energy expended to this end is energy well spent because **the 'why' provides motivation and context.**

#thewhy

What I particularly liked about this approach was that it was seeded by team input and conversations. Our collective thoughts began to distill into some easily understood and relatable elements.

The other exercise we did was a SWOT (Strengths, Weaknesses, Opportunities, and Threats) Analysis. We then word clouded these elements and produced graphics that we mounted and put up in our primary meeting space so that it was a feature in any of our meetings or primary decision-making processes.

We had our Intrinsic Purpose, Core Values, Strengths, Weaknesses, Opportunities, and Threats up on the walls as constant reminders of the clarity we had collectively created and articulated around who we were and 'why' we were in business.

Core Values: A fundamental set of values that drive a business.

Intrinsic Purpose: A statement based on a company's core values that clearly defines the what, who and WHY of a business as well as the goals of its existence.

SWOT Analysis: An internal analysis of a company's Strengths, Weaknesses, Opportunities and Threats in the context of the current marketplace.

#foundation

in·trin·sic
adjective

1. belonging naturally; essential

2. contained wholly within the organ(ization) on which it acts

pur·pose
noun

1. the reason for which something is done or created or for which something exists

2. a person's sense of resolve or determination

When you define your intrinsic purpose, it should encapsulate the ultimate reason for your company's existence. Why it lives and why it breathes. I feel this better encompasses what we seek to achieve than a "mission statement," because it looks deeply into the core of the organization's 'why'.

In this evolving world of conscious capitalism, it is essential to inspire your team with a sense of purpose that serves the greater good.

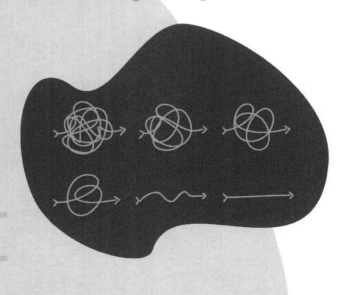

Your intrinsic purpose should chart a course for your company to make a difference. To make positive contributions to the world we live in.

Not every company can be in the clean energy field or producing life-saving products, but if you can tie what you do to the benefit it has to the world at large, this gives your team something larger than a paycheck to be working toward.

When we feel we have a clear and more significant purpose, it can help us get up in the morning and improves our motivation to do our best.

This overarching intrinsic purpose helps bind the individuals in your company into a team and create Affinity, which is why it should be communicated constantly! It needs to be posted, attached, reviewed and reiterated wherever possible.

It needs to be on your walls, in your break room, in the footer of emails, on your business cards, spoken to at meetings, large and small. In other words, it needs to be endemic.

The hardest piece of this, and possibly the most important element, is to keep all the messaging simple, relevant, and in focus.

Focus, Focus, Focus

At one point, I took over the operational leadership of a fitness & wellness company that had a really long mission statement. I knew how incredibly important it was to focus our intent and therefore I encouraged all the team members to learn the mission statement. I offered up a reward for people who could recount it verbatim and had a few people learn it by heart.

During that process, I realized that the mission statement, in and of itself, wasn't really clear and it was unwieldy. The three paragraphs didn't provide real clarity; they actually did the opposite.

We decided to distill our intrinsic purpose down to a sentence . . . which is never easy.

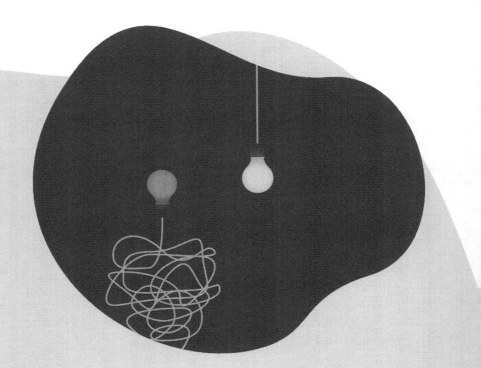

After much debate and numerous iterations, we came up with

"We Change Lives."

Three words that signified the work we were doing in bringing health and wellness to a sector of the market we called the "interested de-conditioned. This intrinsic purpose resonated with the team; it was simple, yet huge. Most of the people working in the fitness and wellness industry innately want to help people and this intrinsic purpose really focused on that desire.

In terms of creating focus and awareness, it is incredibly important to use a mix of media, examples, and events to keep your intrinsic purpose front and center.

In this particular case, we created 'We Change Lives' walls where we highlighted individuals that had seen a significant change in their lives through their own efforts and the efforts of the team.

This distillation of victories brought our intrinsic purpose into focus in very tangible ways.

Additionally, in this group, we had always provided a suggestion box. After a trip to visit other facilities, I had noticed that one of them had a great feedback system called 'Catch Us Doing Something Right'. I loved this conceptually because it was asking members to recognize team members who were helping them, or others, as they went about their day to day duties. It also asked team members to recognize each other's contributions to the whole.

The focus with a suggestion box has usually been to provide an anonymous way for customers to offer up suggestions and oftentimes complain. When we decided to change the format (we called ours, 'Catch Us Exceeding Your Expectations'), something magical happened. Suddenly we started getting all these accolades for our team member's changing lives.

Members were actively looking for and acknowledging the many kind and wonderful things our team members did for them on a daily basis.

It shifted our member's focus from looking for problems to looking for good things happening in their midst. It created positive momentum which permeated the team, the members and the company.

These accolades made it easy to demonstrate why our intrinsic purpose mattered. They made it easy to highlight team members who were making a difference in our members' lives. This didn't stop at the training team, or the group exercise department. We had everyone from our Kidz Zone team to our housekeeping team being recognized and acknowledged.

Linda G. AKA Superstar Team Member

In fact, one of our housekeepers (at the first wellness center we built) received acknowledgment after acknowledgment. We were literally inundated with accolades for her *changing people's lives*. We had a system where we awarded 'stars' to team members who received a . . .

'Catch Us Exceeding Your Expectations'

And with every five recognitions (within a three-month window), team members received a star for their name badge.

Linda, a housekeeping team member of over 20 years who has since retired, received so many acknowledgments of her kindness and care for the members that she quickly ran out of room on her name tag and we needed to create additional tiers for the system to accommodate her outstanding member service.

Linda was the embodiment of our intrinsic purpose. She was changing lives with her kindness in the ladies' locker room and in the lives of every member she touched.

At the end of every year, we would have a team holiday party in each region where our clubs were located and we had awards for team members who embodied our intrinsic purpose and our core values. Linda routinely won the 'We Change Lives' (Intrinsic Purpose) award and even though we tried to spread the awards around the team as much as possible, not a person in the room ever felt like Linda shouldn't get that award.

These very tangible displays help the team focus on what your intrinsic purpose *looks like* and what it means to contribute to it. What I am suggesting is that we speak to and illustrate our intrinsic purpose in simple and meaningful ways to keep it in focus for your entire team.

Side Note About Affinity of Purpose

When Linda first joined our team, she came from a hotel chain, where she had been a housekeeper for almost 25 years. During the course of the interviews, I got to meet Linda and got a sense of the kindness and humility this lady exuded. Over the next few weeks, I would see Linda and say hello and acknowledge her by name. She'd always look at me a little strangely and duck away, seemingly embarrassed.

I put this down to her being shy and didn't think too much about it. After about a month I invited her into my office to see how she was acclimating. I explained I was hearing wonderful things from the team and the members. Again she seemed embarrassed but appreciative of the feedback. As she was leaving, I asked her jokingly if she was scared of me because every time I went up to her and said hello and asked her how she was doing, she seemed really tentative.

Linda explained to me that in over a quarter of a century at the hotel, she had never been personally acknowledged by senior management, and certainly was never called her by her name or asked how her day was going.

She explained that she'd never spoken to a General Manager before and didn't know how to handle me *taking time out of my busy day* for her. That almost broke my heart.

This amazing lady had served people all her life and had for most of her early career remained unacknowledged, and under-appreciated.

Over time, Linda warmed up to me and we became great friends. My appreciation of her contributions only continued to grow. If there was an example of Affinity unfolding, it was happening around Linda. She became a force for good in that club and continued to influence the very fabric of that organization until she retired just recently.

Affinity of purpose isn't created by the appointed leadership, it is created by those that exemplify the principles . . . Linda was an amazing example.

If you provide focus and consistently thread your intrinsic purpose through all things, every team member should have a sense of how the company is making a difference in the world.

In turn, you want to help them connect what they're doing with the company's larger purpose. Drawing that thread through all they do will come in many forms, but with your purpose clearly defined, Affinity will swell through your team and create powerful alignment.

With your intrinsic purpose in focus and the team aligned with that overarching goal, you need to then determine how you're collectively going to get there. It's a given that you want a grand and inspiring purpose to go after, but alignment of your strategy also needs to be debated, created, prioritized and instituted.

I consider the strategy piece to be the 40,000 ft view. It's the major focal point of your operation that contribute to your intrinsic purpose.

In the example of the wellness centers that had the intrinsic purpose of "We Change Lives," one strategic emphasis was on driving deep into the "interested de-conditioned" segment of the fitness and wellness market.

These are the folks that know they should exercise but have not found the right exercise solution. This emphasis aligned well with the intrinsic purpose, because in reaching out to this deep pool of underserved people we were indeed changing lives, significantly.

It also meant we were fishing in a very deep pool of opportunity and there was little to no competition. It was a *Blue Ocean Strategy*.

This was, of course, great for business and aligned perfectly with our intrinsic purpose. This synergy was captured routinely when we'd point out the fact that "You can't change lives you don't touch".

You can't change lives you don't touch.

In the fitness industry, most of the industry competes for the same 15-20% of people that feel comfortable in a health or fitness club. The vast majority of people find that environment intimidating and uninviting. So, creating a place where the *intrinsic purpose* was *to change lives* was, in fact, creating the perfect sanctuary for the uninitiated exerciser to feel welcome.

This is a great example of how the intrinsic purpose aligns with your high-level strategy.

The clubs where we developed this model enjoyed one of the highest market-penetration rates in the U.S., even in the face of growing competition, because our team was aligned in their purpose to change lives and when we invited the uninitiated into our facilities they were greeted with kindness and care.

Amazing team members doing great things for good people.

Most companies will have several strategic initiatives, and these are normally underwritten by a larger number of mid-term objectives. This will be a much more detailed set of goals that contribute to the strategic initiatives, and ultimately the *intrinsic purpose*. These objectives help drill down into the more specific and measurable goals of the company.

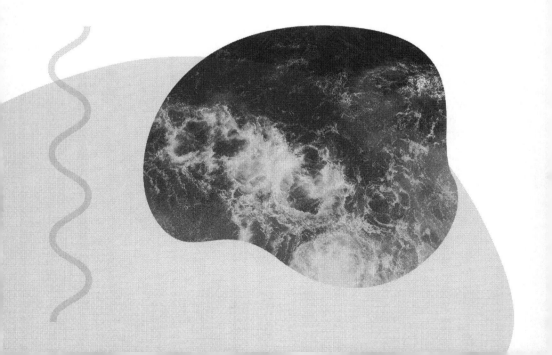

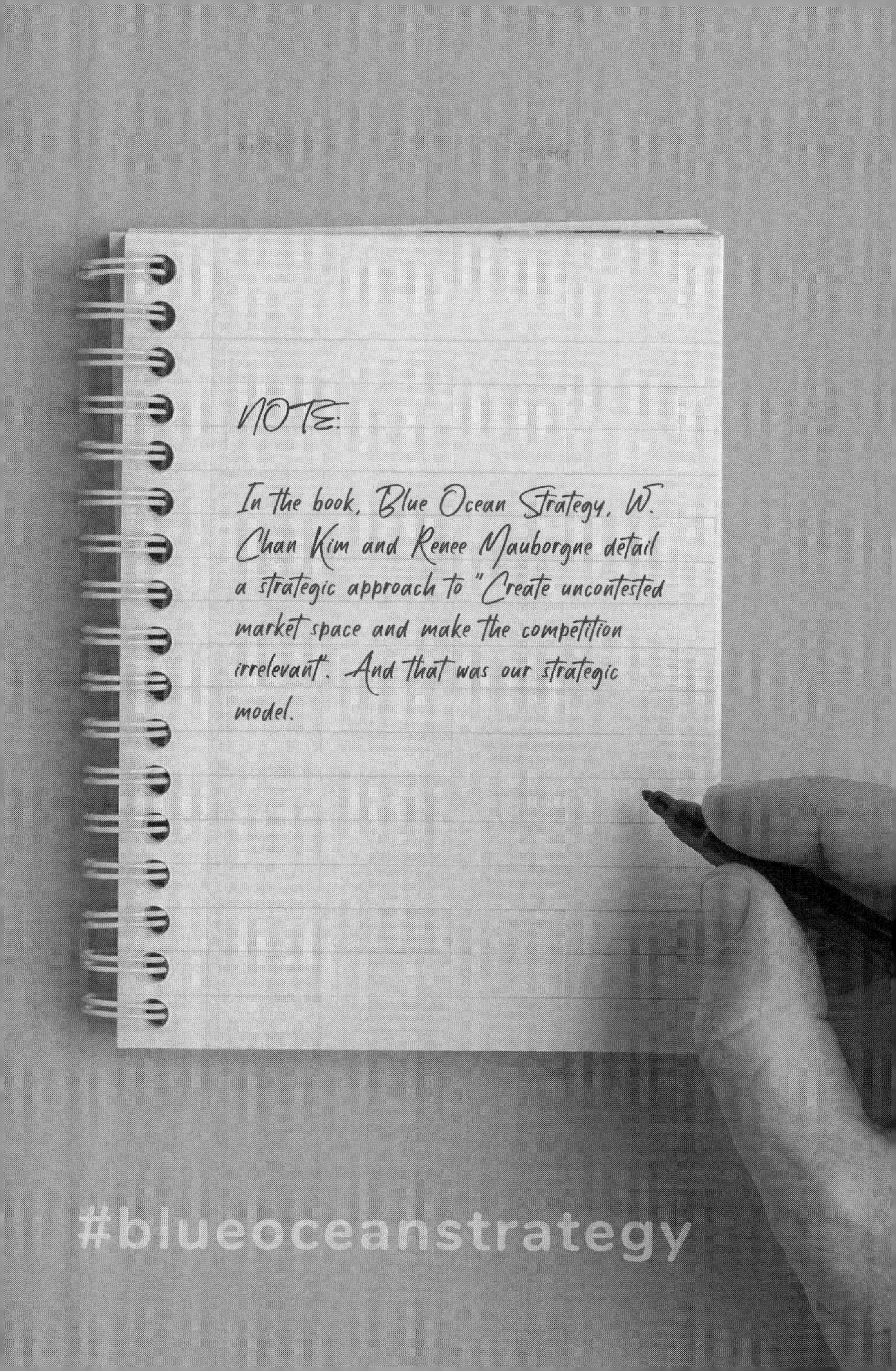

NOTE:

In the book, Blue Ocean Strategy, W. Chan Kim and Renee Mauborgne detail a strategic approach to "Create uncontested market space and make the competition irrelevant". And that was our strategic model.

It is critical that your objectives can be measured and that they align with your strategic initiatives.

An example of a fairly universal objective would be achieving a Net Promoter Score® of XX%.

The Net Promoter Score® (NPS®) measures customer experience and is a powerful predictor of a business's potential growth.

NPS® is something that can be measured in real-time and month on month and year on year scores tracked and relayed to the team. Many things go into creating a great customer experience, and this metric has become somewhat of a standard for customer-facing businesses.

Note & Acknowledgment About NPS®

Net Promoter Score® (NPS®) was developed by Fred Reichheld in the '90s to determine the engagement and brand loyalty of customers.

It was later scaled by Bain & Company, and Satmetrix Systems to become one of the foremost predictors of a company's growth potential.

BRAND LOYALTY

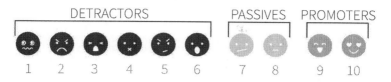

NPS = % PROMOTERS - % DETRACTORS

* Net Promoter, Net Promoter Score, and NPS are trademarks of Satmetrix Systems, Inc., Bain & Company, Inc., and Fred Reichheld

NPS® is simply determined by asking respondents "How likely are you to recommend [x-company] to your friends and family?" and giving them a 0-10 scale to answer.

The NPS® system postulates that every company's customers can be divided into three distinct categories: Respondents rating your company 0-6 on the 10-scale are considered to be Detractors (unhappy customers); 7-8 scores are classified as Passively Satisfied (vulnerable customers); 9-10 scores are termed Promoters (enthusiastic customers).

The overall score is determined by taking the percentage of Detractors from the percentage of Promoters. The respondents scoring 7-8 are considered irrelevant in their influence on the equation.

An example would be 10% of your customers being Detractors (0-6), 20% of your customers being Passively Satisfied (7-8), and 60% of your customers being Promoters. The NPS® would be 10% - 60% = 50% Net Promoter Score.

A '50' on the NPS® scale would be considered excellent for most industries!

Essentially, scoring over 0 suggests you have more loyal customers than disloyal customers, and that's obviously a preferred state.

With strategic initiatives determined and shared; objectives detailed, managed and measured, your company is well-positioned to enhance its Affinity within. It is critical when changes occur to any of these overarching goals or aspirations, that equal attention and energy goes into conveying and reinforcing those changes.

It used to be the norm to have an annual strategic planning retreat that would determine the next twelve months' focus and objectives for a company.

Even though it can be hugely beneficial to bring key stakeholders together, annual strategic meetings need to be complemented by routine and rhythmic reviews of the shorter-term objectives and goals.

This regular focus on the objectives and quantification of progress will help to enhance clarity around your goals and the necessary adjustments or pivots.

The next layer of clarity of purpose and expectations is making the individual team members aware of these goals specific to their function or role.

Depending on the size of your organization, there may be many layers beneath these strategies and objectives but the need to provide clarity should continue relentlessly throughout your organization.

Being clear and specific about the responsibilities and expectations of each individual in their role is a huge undertaking.

Obviously, where roles are repeated this gets easier, but initially establishing who is responsible for each task or objective can be onerous. This can and will change as objectives are reached, goals are achieved, and course corrections take place.

No matter how clearly the lines and responsibilities are drawn and defined, priorities shift, and problems arise.

It is ultimately your responsibility, as the leader, to continue to emphasize the need for clarity as iterations emerge.

Clarity will enhance your team's ability to execute the given mission, and allow your company to shift direction quickly and confidently.

Feedback mechanisms, communication forums, one-on-one conversations, and a continuing obsession for unearthing inconsistencies in the level of clarity within your team, is truly the only way to create Affinity and ensure you get the best out of your team on an ongoing basis.

Perfect clarity through every layer of your organization is an ethereal goal. As you grow and scale, clarity will at times be replaced by ambiguity and you'll need to regroup and re-engineer things all over again. Maintaining clarity in changing markets, amidst evolving technologies and as growth shifts and shuffles is a constant task.

Being a good steward of clarity within your company will bring levels of Affinity most companies only dream about.

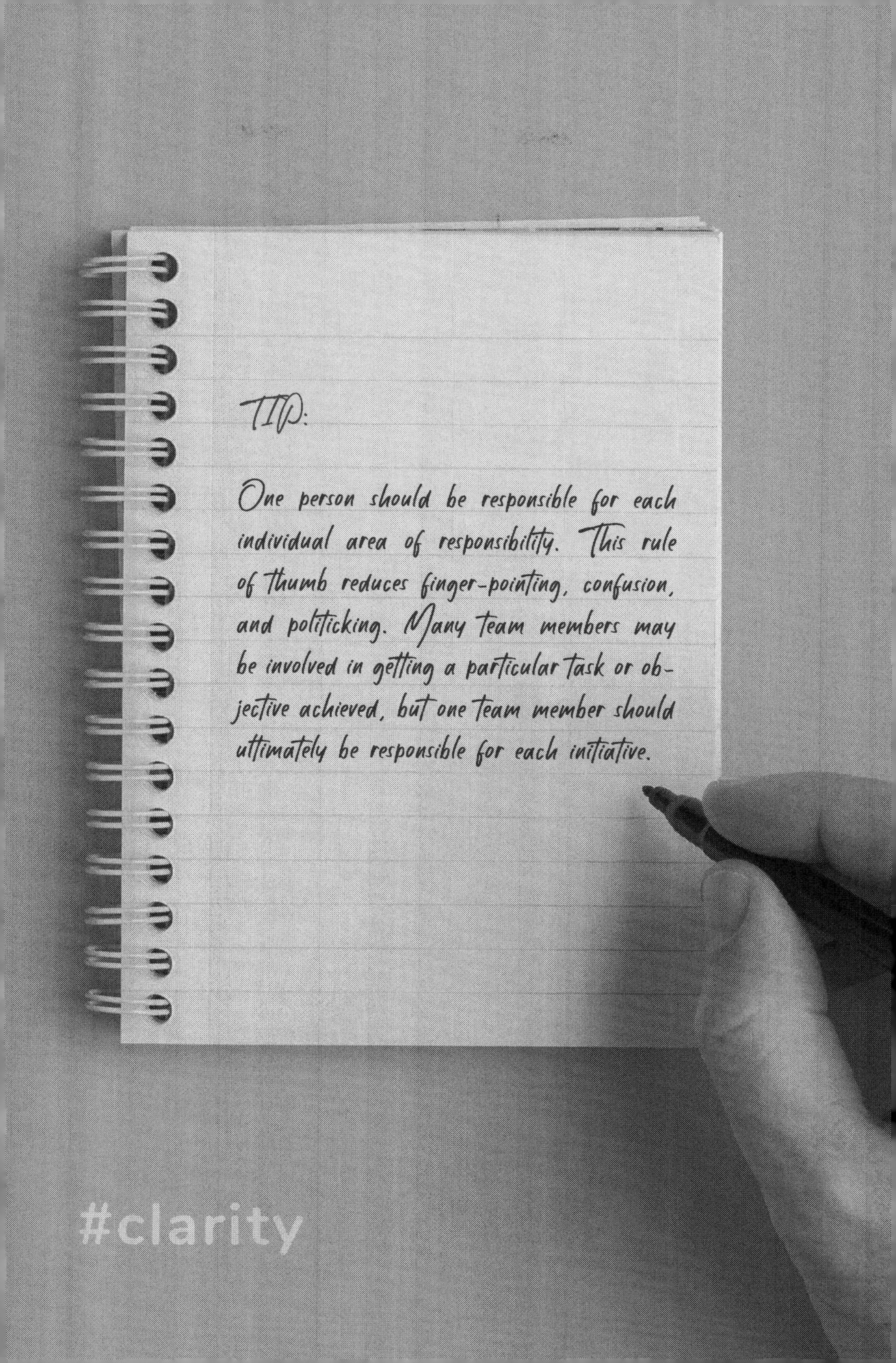

TIP:

One person should be responsible for each individual area of responsibility. This rule of thumb reduces finger-pointing, confusion, and politicking. Many team members may be involved in getting a particular task or objective achieved, but one team member should ultimately be responsible for each initiative.

#clarity

WE RISE UP BY
LIFTING OTHERS.

CHAPTER 12

Encouragement: Raising Your People Up

en·cour·age·ment
noun

1. The action of giving someone support, confidence, or hope

2. Persuasion to do or to continue something

3. The act of trying to stimulate the development of an activity, state, or belief

In creating Affinity, the act of encouraging your team members spreads across all three of the definitions above.

With encouragement comes a sense of confidence and hope underwritten by the support offered in your uplifting words.

Encouragement helps people persevere and in the world of business, perseverance in most things is critical.

However, encouragement is not praise. Encouragement focuses on improvement and recognition of effort and can be doled out liberally in pursuit of the specific outcome sought.

Encouragement also helps create alignment and shape behavior in far more substantial and sustainable ways than disciplinary styles could ever hope to achieve.

Sadly, positive feedback needs to be delivered at a ratio of 6:1 in order to counterbalance constructive feedback. This seems wildly disproportionate, but just look inside and ask yourself how hard you've taken small criticisms over the years and how flippant are about acknowledgments you have received. It is human nature.

We are evolutionary beings and survival is often based on not making the same mistake repeatedly, so we tend to take criticism seriously. It's in our DNA.

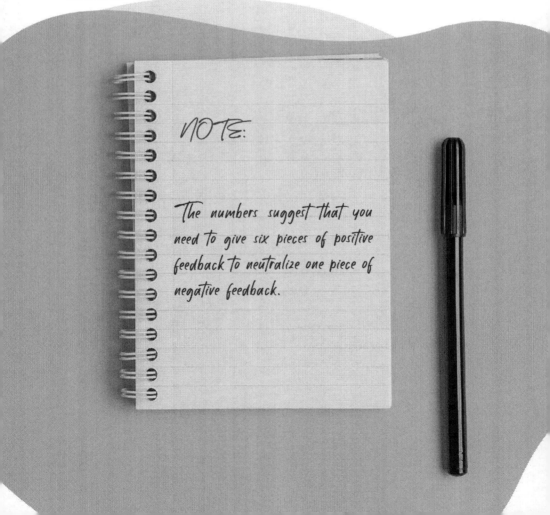

NOTE:

The numbers suggest that you need to give six pieces of positive feedback to neutralize one piece of negative feedback.

Previously, I mentioned the 'Catch Us Exceeding Your Expectations' feedback system we instituted, and I think this tool exemplifies the value of encouragement.

When we position our team members for success and actively go out of our way to encourage others to find them doing good work, we are creating positive momentum and Affinity within our brand.

One of the most fundamentally positive elements of this system, in my opinion, was encouraging team members to recognize and encourage their fellow teammates in their everyday activities.

Your team members can complement your efforts to acknowledge positive efforts on your company's behalf in significant ways. They can help you elevate your team when you're not able!

And encouragement from teammates can be equally, or more rewarding, than encouragement from you.

Finding and recognizing your team members for their accomplishments is a discipline and often not a natural disposition for the more competitive among us. If you aspire to be the best you can be and create a team that has Affinity, then you have a competitive spirit. Equally, you have the capacity to develop the disciplines around success you need to succeed. Encouraging your team is one such critical discipline.

As a competitor, you also appreciate the benefits of encouragement in a coach's style. That is not to say there is no place for constructive feedback in an organization that seeks Affinity. Team members want performance-oriented leaders who challenge the status quo, and that demands continual refinement. Refinement demands course corrections. We just need to ensure that the course corrections do not blur out the positive things that are transpiring as your company pushes toward its goals.

If your style is to manage the minute details then you will likely suffer the fate of clouding the goal from view. When we are being barraged by input we can easily lose focus on the destination.

What I am essentially saying is to balance the constructive feedback as much as possible with positive reinforcement and encouragement.

And as I pointed out earlier, one does not equal one in the feedback stakes. Yet you can't stay on course without giving constructive feedback.

Given that you're going to have to constantly offset those necessary course corrections with positive reinforcement.

This means proactively, and constantly looking for ways to recognize and acknowledge your team members, any chance you get. And a hard-earned piece of advice, "Good job!" won't cut it.

A parenting and coaching lesson I learned was that when you're encouraging teens you need to be specific. They will routinely dismiss that generic bit of praise, "Well done!" or "Good job!" What a teen will likely acknowledge and accept is specifics in reference to their efforts.

And you can't fake it.

This lesson applies equally in the workplace equally as much. I've worked for leaders who have their generic "Atta-boy!" and after a while, these platitudes become white noise and wallpaper.

If you deliver encouragement it needs to be legitimate and specific. Integrity is one of the foundations of great leadership, and false platitudes ultimately fall on deaf ears regardless of how deftly they are delivered.

So how do you deliver all these positive pieces of encouragement when you're deluged by emails and all the trappings of leadership that weigh you down on a daily basis?

Tom Peters talks about MBWA (Management by Wandering Around) in his book *In Search of Excellence*. He presents a great methodology to employ when seeking to catch your team members up to good things. It's also a great way to get up and stretch your legs and see what's really happening beyond the walls of your office.

MBWA refers to a management practice of spontaneous and unstructured visits on team members, departments, and locations.

Because these visits are unexpected, the team members who are focused on their tasks and responsibilities will become apparent (especially over time) and the "show ponies" (those people that wait till someone's watching to make an effort) will equally become evident. The real magic is in gathering regular and robust data points.

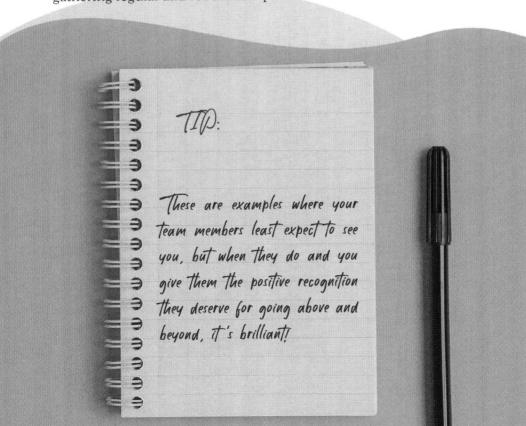

TIP:

These are examples where your team members least expect to see you, but when they do and you give them the positive recognition they deserve for going above and beyond, it's brilliant!

Be aware that random sampling can create some distortions that can only be corrected through continued diligence. MBWA is best applied generously! It is also important to make this non-routine activity a part of your routine.

In other words, you need to get out regularly to visit your team at various times of the day, and night (depending on your line of business).

When I managed businesses that operated 7 days a week, over extended hours, I found that some of the most magical moments happened outside of my office hours. Being greeted by that bright and cheery 'early opener' at 5:25 AM in the morning was a treat. The act of opening the doors of a health club for those early morning exercisers was a delight in the right hands or a disaster in the hands of someone who's not a morning person.

Catching that Manager on Duty jump-starting a customer's car at 10 PM at night was a magic moment not to be missed. The appreciation from that poor soul that had left their lights on probably eclipsed all my platitudes, but just getting to witness these acts of genuine kindness reinforced my need to be out and about catching my team doing great stuff!

When I was managing a company that was shipping tens of thousands of items monthly, my regular visits to the shipping team was likely a welcome respite from the repetitive tasks that team handled, but it always offered great insights for me into the heartbeat of our company.

There are so many intangible benefits to be gleaned from these connections with your team. I have come to appreciate MBWA in all of my leadership roles.

Side Note About Exceeding Expectations

In any business I have led, we have always asked our team members who opened up in the morning to open five minutes earlier than the posted opening time. This is a Disney tradition and I love it. I especially love it because we have all been on the receiving end of the shop assistant, or bank teller, waiting for opening time to roll around on the wall clock (that was typically slow) before strolling to the door to let in their daily dose of frustration.

Sadly, I'm not exaggerating here and most of us have experienced this decided lack of Affinity in businesses we have interacted with over time.

The act of delighting your customers by opening a few minutes early is a small price to pay for a lot of positive goodwill.

Over-delivering obviously needs to be observed with discipline because for the regulars they will come to assume you're opening five minutes early. If that was not made clear to the new early opener, or the sub, you'll get flack even if you opened *on time*.

It is also valuable to express encouragement in meetings or communications with your team when you reach milestones in your journey toward an end goal. These group touches can be very powerful and put context to team-building opportunities. I would encourage you to actively look for opportunities to celebrate achievements and encourage your team members and your team at large.

I am a big fan of huddles and stand-up meetings and use them in a variety of scenarios. Like team meetings, these are great opportunities to recognize team members' efforts on a day-to-day basis.

Mindful, Intentional Communication

A daily stand-up meeting provides valuable insights into other departments, inspiring teamwork, and improved communication, which drives empathy and understanding.

A great example of the value of a stand-up in the encouragement stakes was when I was managing a large multi-purpose facility in Denver, CO. I had been based in Australia at the time and was offered a consulting contract managing the Colorado region for a national group, and also this specific facility.

Unbeknown to me, this facility was affectionately known as "Afghanistan." It was somewhat neglected and had a team that was heavily siloed. I had a dozen department heads and quickly determined that this team was beaten up and interdepartmental communication was inconsistent at best.

I determined that a daily stand-up meeting was needed for the department heads to get everyone talking to each other, and in order for me to shed some light on all the potential we had within this team.

The stand-up model I use is based on one propounded by Verne Harnish.

Each person in the stand-up has 60 seconds to discuss what they did the day before, followed by their plan of action for today, and then any "rocks" they have in their shoes.

Rocks in your shoes are challenges that are hampering you from getting your job done. They do not include generic things like the weather (that might be affecting everyone) but they do include something like the roof leaking into your office onto your computer, for example.

There are guidelines for stand-up meetings, and I enforced a few basic parameters. First was to keep it under 60 seconds because done right, we should take less than 15 minutes for 13 of us to do our downloads if we stick to that rule of thumb.

Another guideline is that the information is for the group. If there's a conversation that needs to be had between two or more parties from the stand-up, they need to have it after the group breaks up.

Additionally, we actually did these stand-ups standing up . . . go figure. Phones were not allowed, no laptops open on desks, we were facing each other in a circle, there was nowhere to hide and no unwanted distractions.

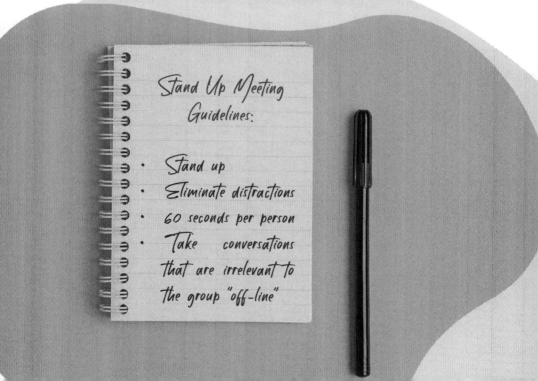

Stand Up Meeting Guidelines:

- Stand up
- Eliminate distractions
- 60 seconds per person
- Take conversations that are irrelevant to the group "off-line"

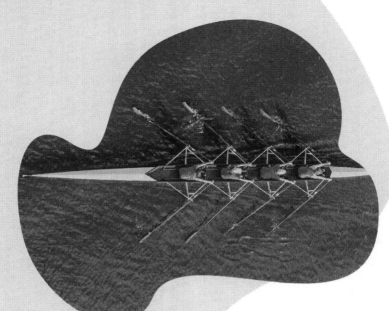

When we started doing these stand-ups, I'm not sure anyone was happy about it. It was 15 minutes out of people's already chaotic day, and initially the team members struggled to recount the previous day's events succinctly. Having a plan for today was not the norm for most of the team, either.

They were simply trying to survive the chaos.

The chaos was there mainly because there was a lack of clarity around roles and a definite lack of communication between departments. Everyone was trying to survive and to an extent, it was every person for themselves.

Soon, however, we started to connect to each other, and I regularly pointed out large and small achievements each team member had contributed the day before, e.g. helping each other achieve a milestone. Affinity began to germinate.

I pointed out and encouraged the behavior that was melding them back into a team and the walls of the silos slowly crumbled. They started to see each other in a more human and empathetic way and appreciated that they were not in this alone.

We each had our rocks (or boulders) in our shoes and every one of us had our plans for the day unravel at times. When we didn't know about something that affected us, there was always the counterpoint where we had failed to inform someone else of things we were up to that had affected them. Communication slowly improved and working together and encouraging each other became more the norm than the exception.

The laughter started to permeate these meetings and camaraderie began to grow.

Not Amazing Today

One of the newest department heads who was probably the least beaten up of the group when I came on board, was a positive beacon that many followed. Brooke was energetic, vibrant and positive . . . about everything. One day, we were going around the circle and got to Brooke. She looked a little under the weather and when I asked her how she was doing, she responded with incredulity,

"I'm not amazing today."

That encapsulated Brooke. She was almost apologetic that she wasn't 110% that day.

This was her family, she hadn't really known things before the stand-ups, and now everyone laughed when she said this. She continued on with her 60-second download, but those sorts of moments defined the development of Affinity in that team. I know that as much as this made us laugh, many of those department heads went out of their way to help Brooke out as she struggled through a day not feeling 110%.

The mutual encouragement and Affinity that arose among that team, over just three months, was amazing. They would recognize each other in their 60 seconds for the help they'd received and the hard work that their team-mates were putting in to turn this facility around.

We planned full days of cleaning and repair days where we scrubbed, painted, and deep cleaned areas that sorely needed a facelift. We cleaned up junk rooms and cleared the cobwebs off vents and trusses. We revitalized equipment that had been mothballed due to a lack of repair. We ignited energy into areas of the club that had languished for years.

Rather than being a place you were sentenced to work, this facility transitioned into a place people wanted to work . . . Affinity blossomed.

And we created this together, encouraging each other all the while. The offers to help, the recognition of each other, the encouragement that grew among this team and their respective teams flowed freely.

In less than 6 months, the club's attrition had reversed, and we began measuring retention growth instead. Sales improved monthly when compared to year-over-year. And programs ranging from Personal Training to Spa services grew substantially, driving additional peripheral income the club had been sorely needing.

I came to appreciate that team so much. They reinforced something that I felt instinctively: that inherently people are good and want to do good work. Sometimes we just need to open up a forum for them to share and encourage each other in order to raise each other up and be our best.

And yes, there will be times when we disappoint each other, but given clarity of purpose, clear expectations, a forum for communication, and the knowledge that you're actively seeking to find the good in people and in what they're doing, your team will rise up.

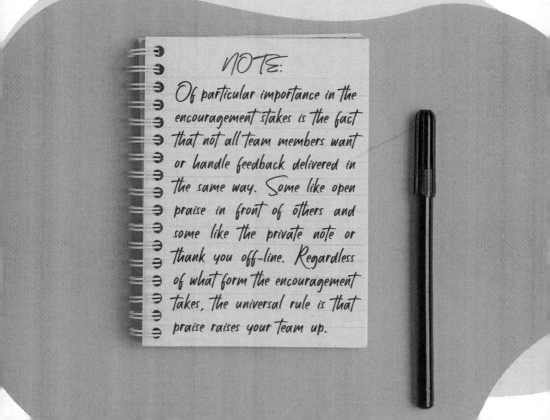

NOTE:

Of particular importance in the encouragement stakes is the fact that not all team members want or handle feedback delivered in the same way. Some like open praise in front of others and some like the private note or thank you off-line. Regardless of what form the encouragement takes, the universal rule is that praise raises your team up.

#flow

CHAPTER 13

Flow State

flow state
adjective

1. An "optimal state of consciousness" where we feel and perform at our best

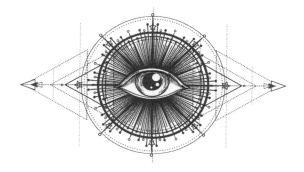

Sometimes described as "fully absorbing experiences," flow states were discovered and named by Mihaly Csikszentmihalyi.

In his book, *Flow: The Psychology of Happiness,* Csikszentmihalyi describes this optimal state where we encounter a challenge that is testing for our skills, and yet our skills and capacities are such that it is possible to meet this challenge.

He also describes how if the challenge exceeds our skills, anxiety will rise. Or if our skills exceed the challenge, boredom sets in. In both these cases where the challenge either exceeds or under-utilizes our capabilities, we're not in a *flow state.*

This quest of Flow applies to you as a leader, to your team members in their daily pursuit of joy in their work, and to your company. When there is a state of Flow Affinity always follows.

Csikszentmihalyi researched a broad spectrum of activities, ranging from work through to sports, and determined that flow is a universal experience. It is something most people have experienced, at one point or another, and is also a changing state.

In other words, as your skills improve, the degree of the challenge must also increase in order to keep you in that flow state.

When a team member is in a flow state in their work, you will see the very best of them. They're performing optimally and they're engrossed in their work. The same applies to you in your work.

When a person, any person, is in flow, time becomes distorted and they wonder where the day went.

Fundamental to harnessing the benefits of flow is to ensure that team members are in the right place, doing the work they're gifted to do. That in and of itself is part of the art and science of leadership. If you can find that team member's inherent gifts that can be applied in your work environment, they'll move into a flow state naturally.

In understanding how to help team members get into this state, we first need to understand the elements that lead to this experience.

There are eight components of this state, of which the first three are non-negotiables and the final 5 are based on the subjective experience of the participant.

8 Components of Flow

1. Clear goals and immediate feedback
2. A high level of concentration on a limited field
3. A balance between skills and challenge
4. The feeling of control
5. Effortlessness
6. An altered perception of time
7. The melding of action and consciousnes
8. The Intrinsic Return On Investment of flow-experiences

#8componentsofflow

▶▶ 1. Clear goals and immediate feedback

Nowhere is this more clearly seen than in sports, where the goals are clear, and feedback is immediate. This is often much harder to achieve in the work environment where there are usually many facets involved in the achievement of a goal, times to goal can be months or years and feedback is often nebulous or non-existent.

This point speaks once again to the need for clarity of purpose and expectations.

Without a sense of what achievement looks like and continued encouragement that defines the right direction, achieving flow is impossible.

This non-negotiable in the achievement of a flow state makes obvious the need for clear destination, stepped and incremental goals and constant feedback.

►► 2. A high level of concentration on a limited field

When we look at the upper echelon of athletes, we realize that focus and concentration in pursuit of excellence is a critical element.

In the often chaotic and contradictory world of business, allowing the individual team member to focus and avoiding constant change of scope or expectations can be difficult. I've worked in companies where the goal has been a constantly moving target and it is impossible to get team members into a flow state when the finish line keeps moving.

Also prevalent in startups and bootstrapping operations is the need for team members to wear multiple hats. As much as this is necessary, in early-stage development, it is also essential to divest these multiple roles as soon as it is financially possible. The beauty of these mixed roles is you can get to see where people flow and where they struggle. This allows you to hire new team members to fill the gaps that have become obvious as you mature as an organization.

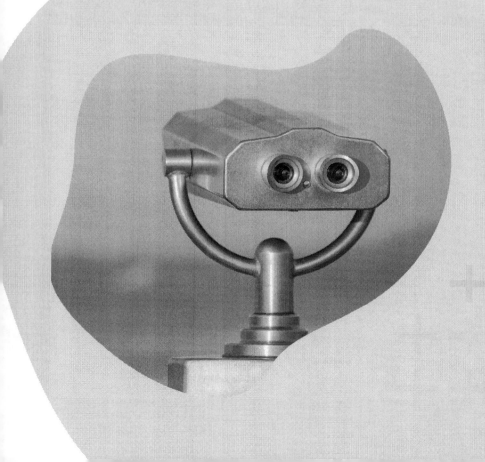

▶▶ 3. A balance between skills and challenge

Music is a great example of this balance. A musician who is playing a piece of music that is too difficult for them will experience frustration and anxiety. In contrast, a piece of music that is too simple will not draw them into that state of bliss when they are sufficiently challenged to realize their full potential.

This represents a constant challenge to leaders in business.

The challenge is to meet team members where their skills align with the difficulty of the task. Yet to constantly challenge and stretch them as their skills evolve.

This band, or *sweet spot*, shifts constantly as they improve their skills and often repeat tasks to the point of distraction.

However, just because someone flows in a particular role, e.g. as a salesperson, doesn't make them the perfect manager. Even though I am advocating for continuing to stretch and challenge your team, moving them up the ladder isn't always the answer.

Continuing to provide growth, learning, and increasing challenges for team members requires a cultural dedication to growth and learning within the organization and this begins with the leader.

⏩ 4. The feeling of control

Characteristic for flow is a state of comfort and relaxation with an absence of stress; described in Zen Buddhism as "control without controlling."

In business, this feeling of control very much relates to the prerequisites of knowing what the goals are, getting constant feedback, and having tools and resources needed, and the opportunity to focus.

When leaders fulfill these non-negotiables, team members have a sense of control and reduced stress. Also making team members aware of Flow will allow them to be aware of their alignment.

Equally, when ambiguity reigns and feedback comes spasmodically, stress rules and flow will be absent.

▶▶ 5. Effortlessness

Flow involves harmony and effortlessness. During the demands of completing an activity, critical decisions occur spontaneously without any deliberate reflection.

This is where the value of guiding team members into a flow state gains traction.

That ability to synchronize with the activity allows them to operate in this optimal state. Performing their tasks and fulfilling their goals seems almost effortless.

Obviously, micromanaging and effortless flow do not mix. When we are allowing team members to align with a flow state, we need to step away and let them flow. Affinity soars when talented team members are freed to do what comes naturally.

►► 6. An altered perception of time

While this is not a non-negotiable, however when in a deep flow-state time often loses relevance. It's a feeling of timelessness. Time can be condensed or expanded in this state. Most of us have experienced this where our sense of time disappears because we are engrossed in an activity that challenges and stimulates us.

From a leader's perspective, when your team is fully engrossed in their designated tasks, productivity leaps. This also improves people's emotional disposition and assists in creating Affinity throughout your organization.

▶▶ 7. The melding of action and consciousness

This is also not a non-negotiable, but complete immersion in an activity can remove fear, distraction, or feelings of self-consciousness. Talented performers experience this oneness with their performance.

This feeling of synergy can expand to a group of people working together, whether that's an orchestra, or your team performing their specific tasks in rhythm and synchronicity with fellow teammates = team flow.

I believe that bringing the right components of a team together demands care and attention of the leader. It is a melding of art and science. The art is the nuance of seeing, guiding, and aligning the right elements of a team. The science is the tools in which you draw on those greater insights for better understanding the complexities of each team member and the blend needed to get a set of tasks done.

ANECDOTE: A wonderful example of the melding of actions and consciousness is in shamanic dancing (see the cover page of this Chapter). This is performed to a "trance-like" beat of drums and the dance is free and unbridled. When dancers become fully absorbed into the dance, they are said to connect with the primal energy of life and often reach "spiritual" states of being, characterized by inner freedom and expansiveness. On a basic level, they enter a state of Flow where their actions and consciousness meld together.

➤➤ 8. The Intrinsic *Return on Investment* of flow-experiences

This element reflects the intrinsic rewards of achievement, or the internal joy in achieving a goal.

This is not a prerequisite of flow, but it is a byproduct.

This further reinforces the need to create incremental *baby steps* toward a larger goal and provide the encouragement to fuel each step.

The beauty of this incremental approach to goal setting is the *Immediate Return On Investment* as each incremental milestone is achieved from a state of flow.

There's a classic Bill Murray movie called, "What About Bob," and one of the key tenets of this movie is "baby steps." As much as we want to take great leaps forward, throughout the history of mankind each great leap forward is typically a function of a whole lot of baby steps. Putting a man on the moon is a classic example.

Creating this state of flow for team members, teams, and yourself, requires leaders to immerse themselves into their teams. The better you understand your team members' gifts, their aversions, their sensibilities, and stress points, the better you can direct them toward their best expression of self at work.

Remember MBWA? The management practice of spontaneous and unstructured visits on team members, departments, and locations I talked about earlier in the book? It is a great way to immerse yourself in your team.

Smaller organizations demand greater care when hiring to ensure that the person fits the role and the company culture, and the role fits the person as ideally as possible.

In larger organizations, you have a little more wiggle room in your ability to move people around to better define the best fit for an individual. When you have a broad array of roles, you can experiment a little and work with individuals more to explore where their state of flow might arise.

I strongly recommend using personality tests, or behavioral strategy assessments, as tools to better understand your team members. Make sure you don't use them in isolation, but merely as data points.

Philosopher Salesman

Eric was the stereotypical *absent-minded professor*. He was brilliant and insightful, but he had also struggled in a variety of positions in an organization I was leading. And yet we believed that he had the fundamental elements that we saw as non-negotiables to our core values.

These non-negotiables are the things that don't usually change in people and can't be easily taught: *great attitude, strong character, high emotional intelligence,* and *positive personality.*

Eric had these elements in abundance, but we hadn't seen his best (or hadn't seen him in Flow) in any of the roles for which he was theoretically suited.

This organization fully embraced Myers-Briggs Type Indicator® (MBTI®, a personality type profile tool), and funnily enough, Eric was actually an MBTI® Master Facilitator (meaning he administered, analyzed, and trained in MBTI®).

Eric tested out in the MBTI® as an "INTP" (Introvert, iNtuitive, Thinker, Perceiver).

Now if you just took that one data point you would likely determine that he is ill-suited for sales. Myers-Briggs suggests that the consummate salesperson is likely an ENFJ, the smooth-talking persuader – almost the exact opposite of Eric's MBTI® profile.

However, Eric kept advocating for himself to try sales. Now an aspect of his persona I respected was his deep self-awareness, so we gave it a try. After moving into the sales role, Eric excelled. He became one of the top salespeople in the organization and later went on to run the sales division for the entire company up and down the Atlantic Coast.

There were several lessons in this experience for me.

Firstly, don't put all your stock in one data point, but gather multiple on which to base your decision.

Also, if someone has the right innate qualities for your organization but isn't excelling in their role, (assuming you have the luxury of experimenting), work with them to try and find the flow state for them.

Another thing I learned was that when a team member is very self-aware, give them some room to explore the areas in which they think they would be best suited.

Lastly, you can employ a *job crafting* approach in some of these circumstances when you can't find the best fit for an individual. Job Crafting gives you an incredible opportunity to create an ideal space for that individual to achieve flow at work.

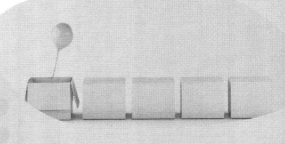

NOTE:

Self-awareness is scarce. Knowing what you don't know, or what you're not suited to, is possibly more important than understanding your strengths.

#knowwhatyoudontknow

Job Crafting

job
noun

1. a paid position of regular employment

craft·ing
noun

1. exercise skill in making (or shaping) something

Job crafting is the customization of a role to better suit the team member's motives, strengths, and passions.

Job crafting ultimately revolves around the team member but must be driven, or underwritten, by the leader.

A key factor in creating Affinity in your organization is having the right people in the right positions. Rigid organizations that can't flex roles and responsibilities have reduced engagement simply because fixed roles and a rigid set of responsibilities rarely acknowledge the differences between individuals.

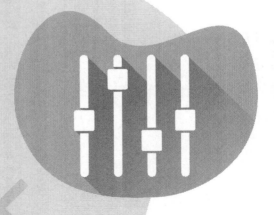

An organization's openness to job crafting stems from leadership.

When leadership allows team members to alter the boundaries, change the nature of their interactions, or alter their own perceptions of a role to suit their innate gifts and particular skills, those team members inherently end up in more of a flow state and the organization, in turn, enjoys the increased Affinity.

This is not a simple, one size fits all solution. Job crafting can leave pieces of a role *leftover* and sometimes overlap roles, where it may need adjustments of another person's role. It can't be thought of in isolation and demands great communication between all parties.

Ideally, when you hire a team member, you're hiring them for the best fit for a particular role. We sometimes learn that our best divinations aren't always completely accurate and we either put up with the rough edges of an imperfect fit or we try and round those edges off. Job crafting is one tool that can help take the jagged edges off a role not perfectly suited to the individual.

The concept of job crafting reflects some of the adaptations the mindful leader makes to a team member's role, and the adjustments the team members make themselves, to create greater job satisfaction, engagement, Flow and Affinity.

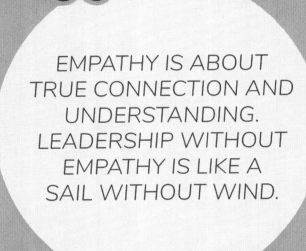

EMPATHY IS ABOUT
TRUE CONNECTION AND
UNDERSTANDING.
LEADERSHIP WITHOUT
EMPATHY IS LIKE A
SAIL WITHOUT WIND.

#empathy

CHAPTER 14

Empathy - Show How Much You Care

em·pa·thy
noun

1. the ability to understand and share the feelings of another

At a basic level, empathy is understanding and relating to the feelings, sensibilities, and motivations of another person.

Empathy requires focus and being truly present for a person. The traits of the empathetic leader have been directly related to team member engagement. How can you effectively inspire and lead someone you don't take the time to understand?

We touched on this earlier and discovered that the empathetic leader creates an atmosphere of trust and increased motivation among their team members. Their empathy can help inspire understanding and appreciation in team members because they feel appreciated; a great example of "what you put in, you get out."

Defensiveness, negativity, and turnover all decrease when empathy is present in the leadership of a company.

Empathy can be developed through mindfulness practices but, in large measure, it often comes from experience and open-mindedness.

The leader who has a true appreciation of what team members do and what challenges they face has the ability to be more empathetic than the leader who has no concept of that particular team member's lot.

It is the norm to empathize with people that are more like us, and that can be very limiting. More importantly, if we only attract team members we empathize with, it will negatively impact our hiring performance.

The lack of diversity in hiring creates a lack of diversity in perspectives within your organization.

Therefore, it is imperative that we practice self-awareness as leaders and actively try to recognize and mitigate our inherent biases. We have to be as open-minded and accepting of differing viewpoints as possible.

When presented with another point of view or a different approach to things, we need to *check our ego at the door* and employ empathy.

When confronted with differing perspectives, it's a good thing to ask ourselves, "Do I have something to learn from this? Why am I resistant to this? What's my motivation for pushing back on this perspective?" If we use simple litmus tests like these, rather than rejecting things out of hand, we will get some valuable input from the other person and ourselves.

A good rule of thumb is to first approach difference with a sense of wonder.

The empathetic leader listens intently and gathers as many data points as possible before making a judgment that affects a hiring decision or another team member.

Listening allows for feedback and the subsequent ability to better appreciate what factors are impacting a candidate, team member or a particular situation. And listening is a cornerstone of a company that has Affinity.

It is important to understand that there are three distinct kinds of empathy: Emotional Empathy, Cognitive Empathy, and Compassionate Empathy.

The elements we are attuned to and vary from person to person and from situation to situation.

Emotional empathy involves really feeling into the emotions of another person.

Really connecting with another person on an emotional level can create a really strong alignment, but it can also be a little intimate for some and needs to be balanced in the workplace.

This is described by Daniel Goleman, author of numerous works on Emotional Intelligence, as emotions becoming "contagious". In other words, you are really feeling the emotions along with the other person. While this can be incredibly powerful, it can also take a toll on you personally and needs to be handled with awareness and care.

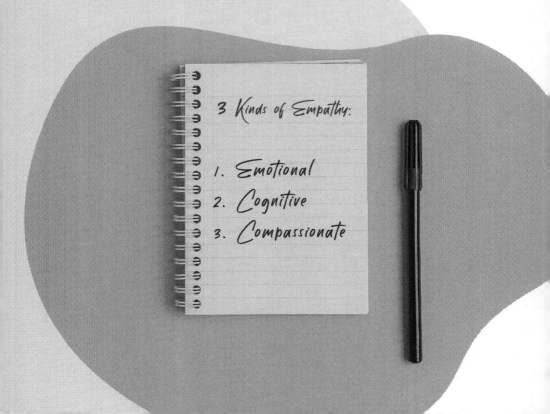

First seek to understand, then to be understood.

-Stephen Covey

On a more intellectual level is Cognitive Empathy. This is typically not deeply felt empathy but does require understanding and thought to connect with the other person and sense how they are feeling.

Cognitive Empathy can help you gain perspective and understand differing viewpoints. This is invaluable in helping to motivate team members and leverage empathy to achieve a goal.

When needing to manage a situation with tact and understanding, Cognitive Empathy is powerful. On the other hand, it can feel a little detached, especially when dealing with emotional circumstances and feelings. It may not feel very compassionate and you may not feel very connected to the other person.

The blend of Emotional and Cognitive Empathy is Compassionate Empathy.

This is where there is not only an understanding and appreciation of the issues and emotions but also a proactive element to the compassionately empathetic response. In other words, in this form of empathy, there is a connection to the feelings being experienced, as well as a desire to help. This creates a powerful balance.

Compassionate Empathy brings the head and the heart together.

This is the space I generally try to move to when trying to relate. The trick is whether to lead with the head, or lead with the heart. Truth is, it usually needs to be a combination of the two and experience, mindfulness and intuition are your best allies. This comes back to centeredness.

In a practical sense, each of us is different and every situation is unique.

Most importantly, what we need to do when cultivating empathy is to be present and gauge the situation mindfully in order to determine how to lead.

In most situations, you'll need both the heart and the head but being conscious will get you closer to the right mix.

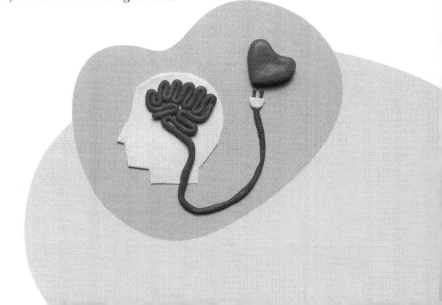

My natural empathy propensity is to lead with the head, so I need to counter this in situations where the individual mainly needs emotional support. My tendency is to be quick to action and oftentimes that can exacerbate the problem. My wife has helped me realize that not everything can be solved with the head, or with a solution.

It is important to remember that gauging what your team members and your organization need empathetically at any given point has an emotional component to it and doesn't just require showing up, it demands that you're present and connected.

It also requires authenticity. Empathy is something that is impossible to fake, and sympathy is not what most functional people want. People want you to relate to them in their circumstances in order for them to feel truly understood and accepted.

Being authentic and communicating effectively is fundamental in showing how much you care.

As in all communications, what you say is only a fraction of what gets conveyed. When you show up with authenticity, your team members will know and appreciate that. For many of us, it takes practice to connect this authenticity to the right facets of our empathy and compassion, to relate to others, and come to understand what motivates or stresses them out.

Don't Overlook the Introvert

I was running a mid-size company and my wife and I would host team parties on occasion to get everyone together. These parties didn't always have a theme, but usually involved food and included spouses.

They gave me a chance to get to know more about our team and their families and I loved getting these additional dimensions of appreciation for the team members I worked with.

When one of our newest team members, Stacy, a big Introvert, came to the first event we had since she joined the company, I was delighted. Stacy introduced her husband, Brian, to me and I quickly realized that he might be even more of an Introvert than her!

I made a point of connecting with Brian and Stacy several times over the course of the party as they tried to blend in. They informed me that his seasonal work had finished up for the winter and he was looking for work.

We were not a company that shied away from hiring family members (provided they weren't in a direct reporting line or the same department) and after my interactions with Brian, my sense was that there was more to this quiet and unassuming young man than met the eye.

My emotional empathy was pushing me to support Stacy, who was an incredible asset to the team and a very hard worker. I had come to know that she and Brian were struggling financially, but my cognitive empathy was intuiting that Brian may be a real asset and that my emotional empathy wasn't completely distorting my perspective.

Fast forward and we had a casual position come up that matched Brian's skills. We hired him very part-time and within a week we knew we had another quiet achiever in our midst.

The moral of this story begins with making the effort to get connected with your team members in different forums. Try and meet their families and make special efforts with those team members that are backward in coming forward.

You'll learn a lot and benefit in perspective as you broaden your sense of who your team member is beyond your normal company bounds.

Those team members that are quiet, private, seemingly closed off, or not easily accessible are often Introverts. They don't thrive in groups but can have a wonderful one-on-one interaction when given them the space to open up. Because I'm an Extrovert by nature, I had not realized these missed opportunities until I was schooled by an Introvert who was also a master of the Myers Briggs personality profiling tool.

Extrovert   Introvert

Extroverts tend to try and fill the void when someone stops speaking, and often process their thoughts by speaking those thoughts out loud. However, Introverts tend to process internally and need time and space to insert themselves into a conversation.

Learning the subtleties of tools like Myers Briggs can have many levels of benefit for developing empathy within yourself and within your company.

In this case, the relationship with Stacy developed because I appreciated that she needed space and time to process. I would deliberately leave white space in our conversations to give her a chance to comfortably express herself. I would also deliberately approach her independently for feedback, not expecting her to come forward in meetings or large forums.

Equally, it is critical to empathize with the extroverts and let them work in groups and collaborate where possible. Give them the opportunity to think out loud and verbally work through problems. They are going to thrive in group interactions, whereas the introvert will shy away from these larger gatherings.

To complete the story, Brian pretty quickly worked his way into a full-time position and proved to be an incredible asset to the company. He is still not the guy to speak up in a meeting, nor is Stacy, but they're phenomenally hard-working people who are making a difference every day, and in their own way creating and contributing to the Affinity in their company. I could have easily misunderstood who they were and how much of a difference they could make if I hadn't been well-schooled in advance.

#listen

CHAPTER 15

Listen - Give Voice to Your Team

lis·ten
verb

1. give one's attention to (someone or something)

noun

1. an act of listening to (someone or something)

Having consulted for numerous nascent, struggling and successful companies over the years, if there was one indelible lesson that carried through every one of those experiences it would be the immeasurable value of communication.

An immense amount of what I garnered from those experiences I learned the hard way. But as my appreciation of the value of strong communications within organizations began to crystallize, I began to leverage this foundational element to create Affinity. With a keen awareness of the value of enhanced communication, performance outcomes improved and Affinity would start to thread its way through the organizations I touched.

I found that one of the most effective ways to enhance communication is simply to listen.

To create platforms, tools, mechanisms and forums for your team to have a voice, and for you to listen . . . intently.

When I talk about tools and mechanisms, I mean two-way exchange systems.

When you give feedback, you should want feedback in return. Equally, when you receive feedback, it's critical to acknowledge that feedback and respond to it appropriately.

If you get feedback that you don't like, it's important to balance an immediate reaction with a considered response.

TIP:

I have worked with a few 'speak to the hand' people throughout my career and when they get triggered, they can demonstrate an inappropriate response to feedback. An individual whose go-to response is 'speak to the hand' will quickly shut down discussions and squelch feedback. If you have someone like this on your team, you have to work diligently with them to recognize their inherent wiring and coach them to take a breath, consider and then consider some more before responding. This is the difference between a reaction and a response, which is far more conscious, mindful and intentional. A great response for these folks when they get their hackles up is, "Let me think about that." A sufficiently non-committal response gives them time to process and review their innate reaction and come back to the person without the bridges between them being ablaze.

#respondvsreact

Review & Feedback Systems

In terms of feedback systems, an area of immense interest to me is review systems.

One of the tools I really like is a self-review system.

This is where the person's position description doubles as their review template. This is powerful because you are reviewing them, and having them review themselves, based on their role. In this system, you ask them to rate themselves on each element of their role and responsibilities. What you're looking for here is their perspective on how they're doing.

You, in turn, do a review based on the same document, which I recommend you do in the same time-frame. In turn, you can review their comments on their performance and they can review your comments, and hopefully, you'll find some common understanding. What is amazing and enlightening is how much this will inform you both.

I've been literally stunned at times with a team member's self-review. I've seen reviews where I felt the team member was being incredibly hard on themselves and this gave rise to a wonderful conversation that gave me lots of opportunities to point out the great things they were doing or achieving. These opportunities are golden.

I've also had reviews where I felt the team member did not have a clear perspective of their downfalls or areas of improvement, I felt they needed to be aware of. But going into the conversation with that perspective gave me such a stronger sense of how to approach it, and that helped the review go more smoothly with that foreknowledge.

Typically, I would spend the initial part of the review asking questions about their responses, almost regardless of where they landed on the continuum. This got them talking, gave them a voice in the conversation, and helped give texture to their perspective. Often, I would find that the team member themselves would give a fair and balanced self-review without me needing to say or inject much at all.

Other times, the difference in perspectives really highlighted gaps in my understanding of the individual, how they were wired, or what they were dealing with on a day to day basis. This is a crucial time to be present and practice high levels of empathy.

I have found the two-way self-review system to be invaluable.

NOTE:

Another element of the two-way review system that I really like is that the person is being reviewed based on their position description. This means what they are hired to do is what is being gauged. This does a lot of things, including bringing the position description up for review as well. Sometimes the team member's role may have morphed since they were hired, and we may have failed to update the responsibilities. Sometimes they are in a completely different role and we have no legitimate basis for the review on the basis of the old position description. These opportunities really help catch and resolve glaring holes in the clarity we are providing and the setting of expectations that may have gone awry.

#twowayreview

The other review system I really like is the 360-degree feedback system.

Having your team review you and the other senior leaders and managers can be incredibly powerful and enlightening.

360s are typically done across the leadership team and confidentiality is the cornerstone of the 360-degree review. Ensuring that the privacy of the team members' comments is upheld is tantamount to this being a valuable feedback mechanism.

I also recommend keeping the focus of a 360 on strengths where possible.

When reviewing the leader's skillsets, issues will appear organically if this system is thorough, and sufficient feedback is garnered. When we're embarking on this journey, we should think about it in the context of the leadership team. As with your team at large, your leadership team should be complementary to each other. It is expected that we can't be good at everything and if we focus on strengths in the 360 review, hopefully, we will see this complementary element come into focus.

This process may also uncover some deficiencies in the leadership team. These are incredible insights and opportunities for you to move your leadership team into new and positive spaces when constructive feedback is garnered from your team in the right forum.

I was a senior executive at a mid-size firm, and we engaged a consultant to do a 360 on our leadership team. This included a detailed behavioral analysis. The consultant we hired for this process met with each leader individually in the testing phase, as well as after the feedback was received from the team and the testing was complete. To me, the best part of the process was when the consultant brought us together as a team and placed all our analyses up on a wall so we could see the crossover, the gaps, and the strengths of our leadership team.

This can be a humbling experience but managed well, it can help optimize your team provided that egos can remain in check.

This is not always easy when you're dealing with high performing and competitive executives.

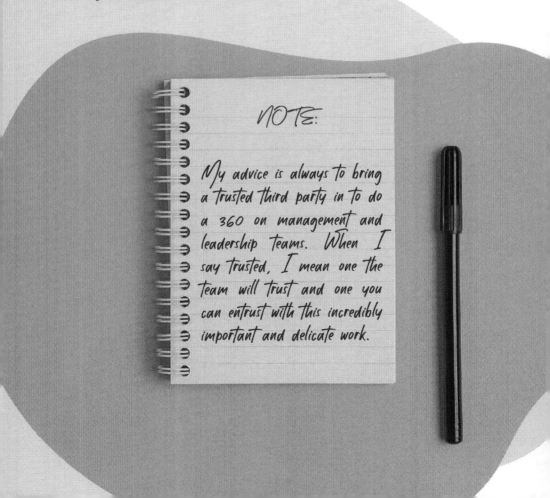

NOTE:

My advice is always to bring a trusted third party in to do a 360 on management and leadership teams. When I say trusted, I mean one the team will trust and one you can entrust with this incredibly important and delicate work.

Open Door Policy

Other platforms for creating forums for your team to have a voice include office protocol. One of my favorites is the open-door policy.

I've worked in open office environments and loved it. I've also worked in highly compartmentalized and stratified environments and did not enjoy it. Some of that was my internal wiring, some of that was the hierarchical nature of the office designations and office etiquette.

When it comes to office environments one type is not going to suit everyone. So, it could be argued that there are no unequivocals. There are great arguments for 'privacy' aiding productivity, but when you work in a productive open office environment or have an open-door policy, trust and *Affinity* are more likely to grow.

By maintaining transparency throughout your work environment, both visually and audibly, trust and morale inevitably improve. Regardless of *why* that meeting, or huddle, is happening behind closed doors, team members that aren't participating in the meeting can sometimes come up with some strange interpretations that stray far from the actual reality.

When you implement a policy like this consistency matters. Not just consistently keeping your office door open, but consistently being accessible. I have encouraged team members to feel they have open access to me, and that I'm accessible, in every office environment I've worked in.

What is difficult at times is creating availability for those people. However, it has always been my goal to keep my office door open whenever and wherever possible and similarly, I have asked my fellow teammates to do the same.

This is not easy for some and does not work for all. Having your door open invites visitors and potential interruptions. When you're focused on writing or you have your head deep in a spreadsheet or research paper, it's tough being interrupted. For the introverts, the quiet alone time of a private space is critical.

Being constantly accessible is challenging in a fast-moving business environment, but the inherent rewards are immense. And truly being present and open to your team visiting when you are in your office will engender trust, respect, enhanced communications, and Affinity.

In my opinion, the trade-off of interruptions over culture is well worth it.

Something that helps open-door accessibility is providing opportunities and tools for your team to get to know each other better. I've managed organizations where Myers Briggs was threaded through every layer of the organization. This was helpful in ways ranging from understanding the Introvert's need for privacy or time to process, all the way through to aligning team members' qualities with their responsibilities.

Knowing Your Teams and Helping Them Know Each Other

I have headed up organizations that have used sophisticated behavioral strategy analyses, and consultants with Ph.D.'s in psychology to better understand the constituent parts of the organization and how they interrelate. I've also worked in organizations with no formal behavioral analyses.

Regardless of the degree of detail and understanding being exacted, the key fact is that the better we know each other in an organization the better we can communicate and accommodate the differences that exist between us. This work helps team members understand that not everyone is wired like them.

Appreciation and Affinity also thrive when empathy and authenticity are blended and threaded through the workplace.

Appreciating and acknowledging team members' differences and nuances, and truly listening, enhances their ability to be themselves.

> True leadership stems from individuality that is honest and sometimes imperfectly expressed . . . Leaders should strive for authenticity over perfection.
>
> -Sheryl Sandberg

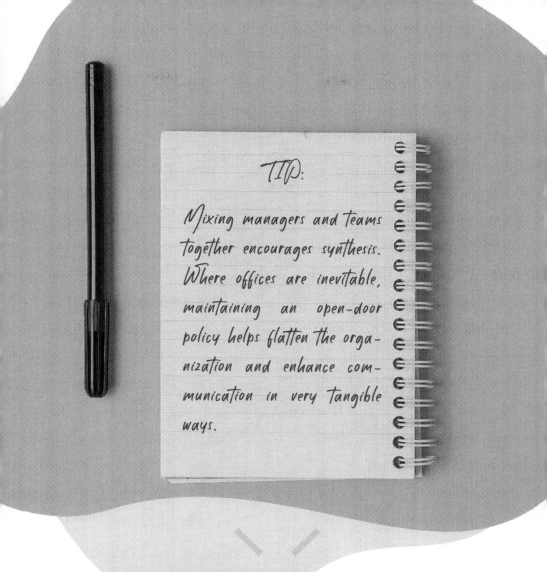

TIP:

Mixing managers and teams together encourages synthesis. Where offices are inevitable, maintaining an open-door policy helps flatten the organization and enhance communication in very tangible ways.

Nowhere does this apply more than to you, as a leader.

When we give your team texture and a voice, amazing things happen. Conversations abound, discourses arise, perspectives change and authenticity thrives. All of this is critical to *Affinity*.

If you think about it, when we create perspective and give voice within an organization, we are really saying let's have discussions and encourage conversations. And I love the definition of conversation . . .

Conversation

con·ver·sa·tion
noun

1. a talk, especially an informal one, between two or more people, in which news and ideas are exchanged

Conversation is about exchanging information and ideas! Sounds like really good stuff can come from that simple idea.

But *healthy* conversations need to be nurtured. This means that a conversation must run in both directions.

I have been in companies where leaders would monologue and pontificate endlessly and the conversation would be sucked out of the room. The basis of a conversation is two or more people having an exchange. A good rule of thumb for a meeting is everyone should have something to contribute to the conversation, otherwise, they probably shouldn't be in the meeting.

How to Keep the Conversation Going

Firstly, don't monologue.

Even if you're the smartest person in the room and believe you have the most to add, or have some great point to pontificate upon, resist the urge. A great mentor of mine once told me that I needed to talk less in meetings. He was very generous in saying I might have the most to add, but he was right. I wasn't always leaving space for others to share in the conversation. From that point on, I focused on trying to open the room up and avoid trying to have all the answers.

Another great conversation catalyst is asking open-ended questions.

By encouraging people to put texture into conversations or meetings, we broaden understanding and stimulate communication. It's easy to get a *yes* or *no*, but when the question demands more, you will typically benefit greatly from the additional input.

Another great rule of thumb in conversations or meetings is brevity.

Keep it short and to the point, which also allows you more time to listen. I personally love the concept of the elevator conversation. Not everything can be distilled into 15-30 seconds, but these small powerful sound bites gain far more traction than a long-winded thesis that leaves everyone's eyes glazed over and reaching for their phones.

On that note, avoid distractions during a conversation or a meeting.

Nothing signals your lack of presence or lack of interest in a conversation, or in the person speaking, more than checking your phone. We've all been guilty of sneaking a peek at that text that just pinged us, or checking our email Inbox. We need to ensure that we and our team follow good phone and laptop/tablet etiquette during meetings.

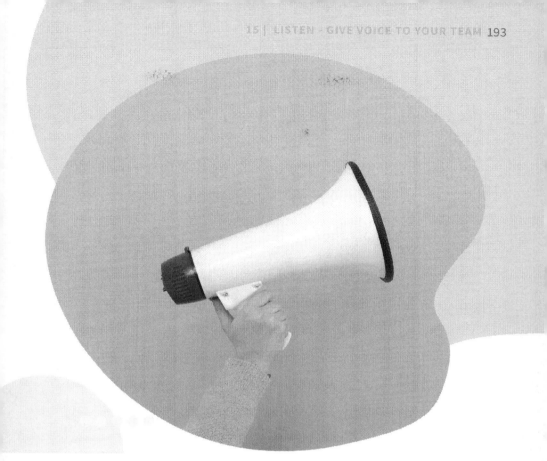

Keeping it short and sharp is also far more powerful in a conversation or meeting when you have a point to make, early in the conversation, or at the front end of your presentation. This is the case because we humans have an incredible filter system that cuts in as early as 8 seconds into a conversation. This filter system helps protect us against the deluge of input and mental stimulation we're receiving almost every waking moment.

This filter is amplified by a growing wave of attention deficit disorders that almost demand that we make our point early in the conversation or presentation if we want to be heard. This also helps if the meeting or conversation gets sidetracked along the way.

To complete the thought on phones: cell phones are critical digital communication and informational tools these days, providing more computing power than many supercomputers of yesteryear. But they also routinely undermine quality analog communications between people.

Digital vs. Analog

I was in an analog recording studio several years back and was taken by the warmth that emanated from the tubes and dials of this 'old school' technology. Most music that I was listening to at that point was digitally recorded and I was amazed that even the electric guitar's sharp edges were being transformed through an old Marshall amp. This experience gave me a new appreciation for 'analog' . . . the warmth of the wave.

On an oscilloscope (displays analog electrical signals), a digital 'waveform' would appear as a series of blocks, much like a digital picture is a series of blocks, or pixels (lots of hard edges). On that same oscilloscope, analog waveforms have curves; soft, beautiful curves. We, humans, are also made up of these same soft, beautiful curves . . . we are analog beings, in a world of digits and pixels.

The parallel to our digital world has broad and significant ramifications. On the simplest level, it is the difference between a handshake or a hug versus a smiley face emoji pumped through the ether.

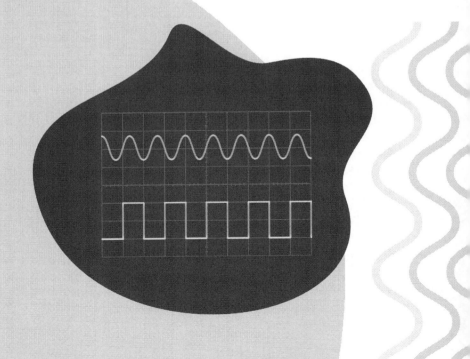

There's no ignoring the onslaught of the digital age in our work, our relationships, and everyday life, but we do need to remember that the energy flowing through us, the energy that defines our very being, is analog.

This was highlighted for me at a company I was running some time back. I was down on the shipping floor checking in with our shipping manager. The phone was ringing and she looked at the phones' screen and expressed her exasperation, "I wish they'd just walk down here sometimes, rather than calling me all the time! They're literally fifty feet away in their office!"

What difference is there between that person in their office calling her, or them walking down to her station? Isn't it more efficient to just call? I'd contend that we lose a lot in that digital transaction! Firstly, if that person got up and out of their office, they'd benefit from a screen break, some light exercise, and a change of scenery. And both parties would benefit from an analog interaction. Unquestionably, the rewards of that in-person transaction almost always exceed the benefits of the digital alternative . . . on so many levels. The effort made is usually returned many times over.

And truth be told, this analog 'transaction' cannot be replaced by a digital 'exchange' because it immerses that person into their counterparts' world. On the most visceral level simply being in the same space as the other person creates an energy exchange that cannot be replicated digitally.

It's almost impossible to be empathetic to the hustle and bustle of a busy shipping department when you're not immersed in it. And it certainly gave me a heightened appreciation of how hard that shipping team works, every time I would step out of my 'corner office' and walk down to their station, as opposed to picking up my phone and dialing their extension.

A graphic example of this is during the peak of summer when most warehouses become pretty harsh environments for those teams that inhabit them. When you step out of your air-conditioned office and walk out 'onto the floor' (especially on those unbearably hot days), your empathy soars with the temperature.

So how is this applicable to us in our day to day transactions?

I believe it is applicable on every level, and in every aspect of our lives.

In a time when depression is rampant, chronic disease and viruses are spiraling out of control, working from home in isolation is more the norm, our environment is under threat, and we're struggling to keep up in these tumultuous times, true community and analog connections are more important than ever.

Let me drop this down to the most fundamental level, and how this analog approach can benefit you in your relationships and communication in general.

In many studies of those communities that defy the norm in longevity, the community is the No. 1 cited contributing factor to the extraordinary lifespan those community members enjoy.

Those communities are tight-knit; they have deep support systems and social underpinnings, they have Affinity that thrives in the analog experience.

The community members meet in the town square, in their churches and their pubs, they visit each other for no particular reason, or specifically because they know that a community member needs their help. It is a constant and consistent analog experience. On a quantum level, their energies are interlaced, they share and redistribute their energy, their energy flows freely through the community, and is not isolated and fractured by the human silos we create in the digital world.

This 'community' experience cannot be replaced with a text, a Tweet, a Snap, or a Facebook or Instagram post. It cannot be replaced over a phone line, or even on a Skype call.

I am not railing on social media or even the digital age, but I am drawing a direct line between our need for true community and connections on a visceral level and the health of our very beings. I am also drawing a direct correlation to the health of our homes, communities and workplaces. In fact fostering a sense of community in your company may be the single best way to grow Affinity.

I realize that an in-person transaction is not always practical. Visiting your workmate 'in-person' might well involve plane trips and a Lyft ride. That's the way of our decentralized and compartmentalized world. But if we're aware of the importance and ramifications of these opportunities to actually get face to face with others, we will be rewarded physically, emotionally, and spiritually!

Those in-person connections, transactions, conversations, and opportunities are not simply important, they're essential for our well-being. I'd go so far as to say they're critical to the long-term health of our species, and our planet.

Truth be told, every day we pass up opportunities to walk across the hall and check-in with a workmate, or pop our head into our kids' bedrooms before they go to sleep, or take a break and have a coffee or lunch with a friend who's struggling. We choose to grow our community through Linked In or Facebook, to message each other or send an email, while our analog contacts continue to diminish at an alarming rate.

A graphic example is our teenage kids. They're friends with kids they've never met in person, that oftentimes they will never meet. They're stuck in their bedrooms building a digital community while they struggle to have a face to face conversation with peers at school. It's torture for them to look an adult in the eye, let alone shake their hand with confidence. This is not healthy for them, it's not healthy for our relationships with them, it's not healthy for our communities, or our future.

Whereas digital interfaces have become extensions of our community, I contend that pixels and digits should not define us, nor our future.

The challenge is to rejoice in our humanity. To get out of our offices, replace that phone call with an in-person visit, have dinner with our kids (at the dinner table sans phones), meet our neighbors, and consciously build our analog community!

In short, revel in and nurture your analog nature!

Analog Meetings

People joke about getting their cell phone attached to their anatomy because it is a very real extension of who they are today. As much as phones permeate almost every waking moment of our lives, they can also create a chasm in our communications. If we consciously put the phone aside and create space to listen, intently, in conversations between workmates, friends, and family you'll be amazed at the things you hear and the messages you get across.

I would also extend this recommendation to laptops and tablets. It's commonplace for people in meetings to be tapping away on their laptops or tablets. It's equally commonplace when meeting with someone in their office for them to have a screen between the two of them, or off to the side. It's also almost the norm that they'll have their attention drawn away from the other person or people to the screen to check on an email or such.

I can speak with authority on this because I have caught myself doing exactly that. Ads I became more and more aware of these distractions I developed the habit of stepping away from my screens and getting face to face with the team member who had come into my office. In my most recent corporate role, I had a small conference table in my office and this was my favorite place to meet with people because I knew I wouldn't get distracted by the inevitable gravitational pull of the screens on my desk.

In my opinion, the rule of thumb should be no screens when we're one-on-one, or in meetings.

Not always feasible, but I know the quality of the exchange, the enhanced listening ability and subsequent increased level of Affinity makes the digital separation a worthwhile exchange.

And when it comes down to it, one of the best ways to show respect, appreciation, and grace toward another is to be present with them and listen to them with undivided attention.

Multitasking

Having worked in chaotic work environments, as well as in well-oiled machines where structure ruled, I have come to realize that multitasking is a misnomer. Especially when dealing with word processing, which is a lot of what we tend to do in management and leadership roles.

The simple fact is that we can usually walk and talk at the same time (I love walking meetings), because we are using different parts of the brain for those two distinctly different tasks.

Jonathan Cohen at Princeton University has shown in his lab that we do better at two tasks that are less similar, but struggle more when the tasks are very much the same.

So when we are in a conversation and a text comes through on our phone we have to give up some comprehension in one or both of the exchanges.

Equally, when your phone or laptop informs you that you have an email, your brain shifts some of its processing power over to wondering or assessing what that email might be about and maybe reading the subject line. While we're paying attention to those internal machinations, or reading the subject, it's difficult to keep our focus on the person or task in front of us.

I know people who insist that they can split their attention between multiple word processing tasks and retain equal capabilities on both tasks.

Research suggests that less than 2% of people have the ability to multitask. Typically, one or more likely both, of the exchanges will be compromised and comprehension and retention will suffer as a result.

And when it comes to listening to our teammates, peers, customers and other stakeholders in and around our business, our ability to stop and focus on just one thing at a time (to be totally present for that exchange) will reward us with comprehension, retention and most importantly Affinity with that person or people in the exchange.

Rising to Challenges with Vulnerability and Authenticity

So, if you're really present and listening to your team, what happens if you hear something you don't like? Or maybe it's a tough question you struggle to answer?

When you're tapped in, the feedback you're going to obtain, opinions you're going to hear, and questions that will be posed can at times be downright confronting.

It is especially difficult for the leader to be challenged when we're supposed to have all the answers. Especially in public. There is a vulnerability that this creates and an authenticity that is demanded.

I also think these moments are defining.

Our ability to accept alternate opinions, brave criticism, and inspire debate, will not just improve the quality of the feedback we receive, it will enhance the trust and respect we attract from our team and inevitably build Affinity.

Differing opinions, expressed without fear of reprisal, will also promote creativity.

But that is tough! Listening to contrary or negative opinions is counter to how we're innately wired.

Professor Francesca Gino, from Harvard Business School, has shown that we tend to gravitate to people that agree with us and attract people that are like us. This can be a major flaw in hiring and very definitely reduces the breadth and depth of data points we are going to receive within our organization.

Professor Gino's research shows that when we seek opinions from people that might disagree with us, or that are from outside our inner circle, these alternate views and possibly negative insights, often lead to significant improvements in the outcome.

Much like a GPS, if we gathered all our data from one type of data source the accuracy of our positioning or perspective would be naturally skewed. A GPS requires three data points from three separate locations to be accurate and similarly if we seek multiple data points from disparate sources the accuracy of our perspective will be enhanced.

Having everyone agreeing with you in meetings and at the Boardroom table may work in very limited scenarios, but if you have a growing business, fighting for space in the most competitive marketplace in human history, we need as many perspectives and as much brain power and collective genius applied as possible.

One way to instill this fearlessness in your team is to openly embrace differing opinions. Listening to and entertaining these counter opinions is a great place to start.

The degree of open-mindedness you demonstrate in discourse will determine the speed at which the voice of your team will rise.

At the end of the day, the buck does likely stop with you, and if that is the case and you decide to go in a direction counter to the discourse, you need to communicate your reasoning and accept that you may hear an occasional "I told you so" if things don't pan out as planned.

As I discussed earlier one of the key attributes that a high performance team is looking for from their leader is decisiveness. Ultimately, you're making decisions that need to take into account a number of different stakeholders . . . so listen, process, decide and move. Regardless of the outcome, if you've really listened to the voice of your team you'll make a lot more right decisions than wrong ones and you'll enjoy the support of your team because they know you're listening and you're all in this together.

#vulnerability

CHAPTER 16

Vulnerability - Embrace 'You'

vul·ner·a·bil·i·ty
noun

1. the quality or state of being exposed to the possibility of being attacked or harmed, either physically or emotionally

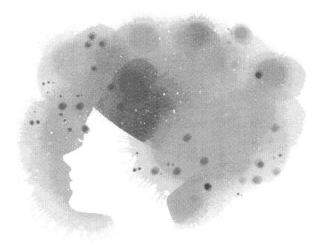

In the previous chapter, I talked about attracting team members who may have alternate views to you. On some levels, this can evoke a feeling of vulnerability. When we're surrounded by like-minded people seeing the world the way we do, there's a certain comfort in that camaraderie.

Yet as we open ourselves up to differing opinions without fear of vulnerability, we become more resilient. We must understand that we don't have all the answers and allow for additional points of view to permeate our bubble and confront the inevitable confirmation bias we all have.

Vulnerability is implicitly linked to authenticity.

Finding the balance between authenticity and oversharing relies heavily on your emotional intelligence. You can't script vulnerability, or act it out. Your team members will intuit a lack of authenticity and it will backfire on you.

Being vulnerable and relatable with your team should enhance your relationship with them. Being real and exposed should open you up to your team and not put them on edge.

Vulnerability is not about oversharing intimate details, it is about creating trust and building relationships. It is about resonating with people. And those things don't happen instantly or in-authentically.

Vulnerability is not about evoking pity. The goal of being open, authentic, and vulnerable is to be accessible, not to elicit sympathy.

One way to determine whether or not your transparency is coming from the right place is to determine if it is helpful to your team members.

If the benefit of your sharing something is useful and your team can learn and benefit from that openness, then that's where vulnerability is valuable in the workplace.

> *Vulnerability is not winning or losing. It's having the courage to show up and be seen when we have no control over the **outcome**.*
>
> -Brené Brown

Sweat, Tears, Vulnerability & Authenticity

One of the greatest points of vulnerability in my career happened when my wife and I were living in Brisbane. Our two young kids, Jack and Ellie, weren't even in school yet and I was consulting with a large firm in the fitness space. An opportunity came up to purchase a small health club chain in Brisbane and after much debate, we decided to go for it. We had spent a lot of time doing our due diligence and even though the business was losing a moderate amount of money every month, based on my experience and projections, I believed that we could turn it around fairly easily.

On our first day working in the business, we started answering the phones and there was call after call from frustrated members who had canceled their memberships months before and were still getting billed. It turned out that there were hundreds upon hundreds of members being billed that had asked for their membership to be canceled, often repeatedly and for months on end.

So, on paper, the business was losing a moderate amount, but in actuality when we canceled all these entrapped members the business was losing a seemingly insurmountable amount of money every month.

We had budgeted for losses, but not at this cataclysmic level . . . we were completely vulnerable.

It appeared that the General Manager of this business had been holding these cancellations over because he was commissioned on the monthly billing income. The sellers claimed they had no idea about what was going on and were not prepared to accept any responsibility. When we spoke with our attorney, the advice we got was that we would need a lot more money than we had to battle this out in court, given the Seller's deep pockets.

Facing the harsh reality of *do or die*, we went to the team. We had come in with a lot of confidence in our ability to turn the ship around, but I now had to go to the team and tell them that I was unsure of our ability to navigate out of this mess. I explained that I would approach the landlords and appraise them of the situation and ask for some grace over the foreseeable future.

I mapped out our strategy, which involved a huge tightening of belts, curtailing some of the grandiose plans we had for the clubs, and my wife and I would be working an inordinate amount of hours to fill the gaps. We also committed to doing a lot of the renovations and improvements, we felt were non-negotiable, with our own hands.

The team took this news relatively well. We'd been very transparent with them from the outset and had given them no cause to doubt me to this point. We were incredibly vulnerable and I believe they genuinely appreciated the predicament we all faced and they agreed to do their collective best to help us get the ship back on course.

We then had to go to the landlords and admit our financial vulnerability. After all my assurances that we had a really strong strategy and the money to execute the plan, we were going back, cap in hand. Based on what I now knew, our cash reserves would be stripped dry in less than 6 months. I think the fact that I was completely transparent with them and incredibly vulnerable as a result, both landlords agreed to work with us . . . that was at least a start.

Then to cap all this off, the flagship club in the city underwent a rezoning of its free parking spaces, and what had been almost 170 free adjacent on-street parking spots suddenly became metered, charging inner city rates. Some members simply quit while most others had to question if they'd keep their memberships due to the high parking rates. They didn't really know us and they relied on these spots for their workouts. We were down to ten free parking spaces for members for the majority of the week.

What ensued was the toughest 18 months of our lives.

We put in all of our liquid assets, sold our house and everything that wasn't bolted down, I cashed in my retirement policy, we took out a second mortgage on our home back in the States and now our mortgages exceeded the rent we were getting on that house. So, we subsisted on the minimum draw possible in order to put everything back into the business. We often went to the grocery store wondering if we'd have enough to pay for that week's groceries.

Our kids, who at the time were 3 and 4 years old, spent a lot of time at the clubs while we worked and my wife took the majority of the burden of their care and on top of the financial, physical, and emotional stress, that took a tremendous toll.

My wife, Jana, took on marketing and taught herself graphic design. Her innate marketing gifts helped push the clubs in the right direction and in her spare time she worked in the day spa, worked reception, painted walls at night and on the weekends, and took care of two little ones.

NOTE: Jana has since started up her own marketing and branding agency and has employed her gifts to help other businesses rise up.

I was running constant defense trying to juggle the creditors, keep all stakeholders informed and intact, and squeeze every cent out of the operations. On weekends and every spare minute, I donned the tool-belt and did demolition work and rebuilt spaces to optimize our rentable space. We added kids' amenities and rentable spaces and each little increment helped.

As we drew closer and closer to break even, it seemed harder and harder to cross that line. I would stare at the numbers almost trying to will them over the line. I took to going door to door to survey the market and canvas potential members. We spent every waking hour working on the clubs and in the clubs but time was running out.

The landlords had been incredibly reasonable, but their patience was not without bounds. At this point, the team had not missed a paycheck, but we had asked a lot of them. They helped us with the kids, they worked extra hours, and they gave their very best even on the worst days. They had become family, but as such, they were in the inner circle and knew we were fraying at the edges.

When things get this frayed, Affinity seems unattainable. We had felt like we were swimming up a raging torrent, not flowing with the current. But at all points we remained open, transparent, and subsequently vulnerable. We learned that Affinity can rise around you even when you least think it possible.

In the end, I had to take a second job to cover our rent and groceries. We had completely run out of cash reserves. With me working a second full-time job and traveling overseas one week a month, that left the majority of responsibility for the clubs and the kids on my wife who was exhausted and beyond frustrated with the predicament we found ourselves in. We were completely vulnerable emotionally as well as financially.

Throughout this saga, we put it all on the table. Our hearts, our souls, and literally everything we had to offer. We were completely vulnerable from day one until the day that we started to break even. Eventually, we ended up selling the businesses as profitable enterprises almost two years later. By this time, we had accrued so much debt that we walked away completely empty-handed and exhausted.

The lessons from this time are etched in my psyche and when we reflect on how we got through it all, we come to the conclusion that it was a lot of things, but most of all it was the Affinity we had created with our team and the frequent and transparent communication we had with our landlords, stakeholders, and creditors.

The genuine vulnerability that we had exhibited throughout these trials and tribulations had instilled trust and helped align the power of Affinity.

We had sought the team's help, their counsel, their support, and received it in return. I think in large measure because of the courage we displayed when we shared the predicament that we found ourselves in.

Jana and I look back on those days and marvel at the fact that we survived. And there is no doubt that the humanity of the situation, the shared experience we had with the team, created the Affinity I reference throughout this book.

Brené Brown, an expert on social connection, argues that vulnerability and authenticity are at the root of all human connections.

Merely projecting an image is not sufficient, it is the transparency you exhibit that resonates with our subconscious to allow empathy and interaction to be enhanced. I strongly recommend all of Brené's work to anyone trying to be a better leader or just a better human.

There are risks, however. When we open ourselves up, we can feel exposed and at risk, which is the very definition of vulnerability.

The authentic and vulnerable leader is also empathetic and because they are aware of and willing to admit their own frailties, forgiveness comes easier to a vulnerable leader.

Forgiveness in turn breeds trust, engagement, and ultimately, Affinity.

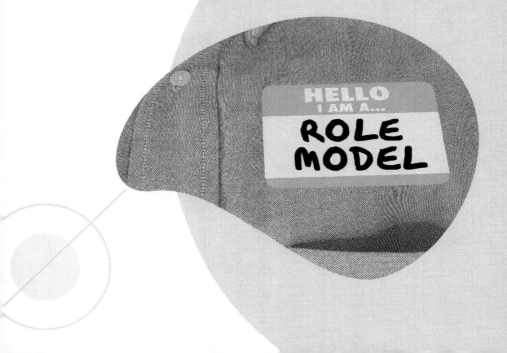

In studies by University of Michigan researcher, Kim Cameron, Kim has shown very tangible upsides for forgiveness in the workplace.

Cameron points to hard data showing that team member productivity and voluntary turnover decreases as a consequence of a culture of forgiveness.

The old paradigm of the tough, unforgiving and uncompromising leader, who can do no wrong, has been proven to be flawed over and again. Endless research points to authenticity, and in turn vulnerability, as the resonant frequencies that our humanity aligns with.

Our bodies respond viscerally to inauthentic people and the hierarchical structure can only raise the leader as far as their title allows.

As much as we may have to bend to the will of the leader's title, John C. Maxwell points out in his book, "How Successful People Lead," that the pinnacle of leadership has nothing to do with the title and everything to do with who you are and what you represent.

Maxwell describes it as Level 5 Leadership. The Maxwell model illustrates the Levels of Leadership and is one of the most succinct and accurate guides to the ascension of a leader that I have come across.

To be a Level 5 Leader, one must be both authentic and vulnerable.

John C. Maxwell's
5 LEVELS OF LEADERSHIP

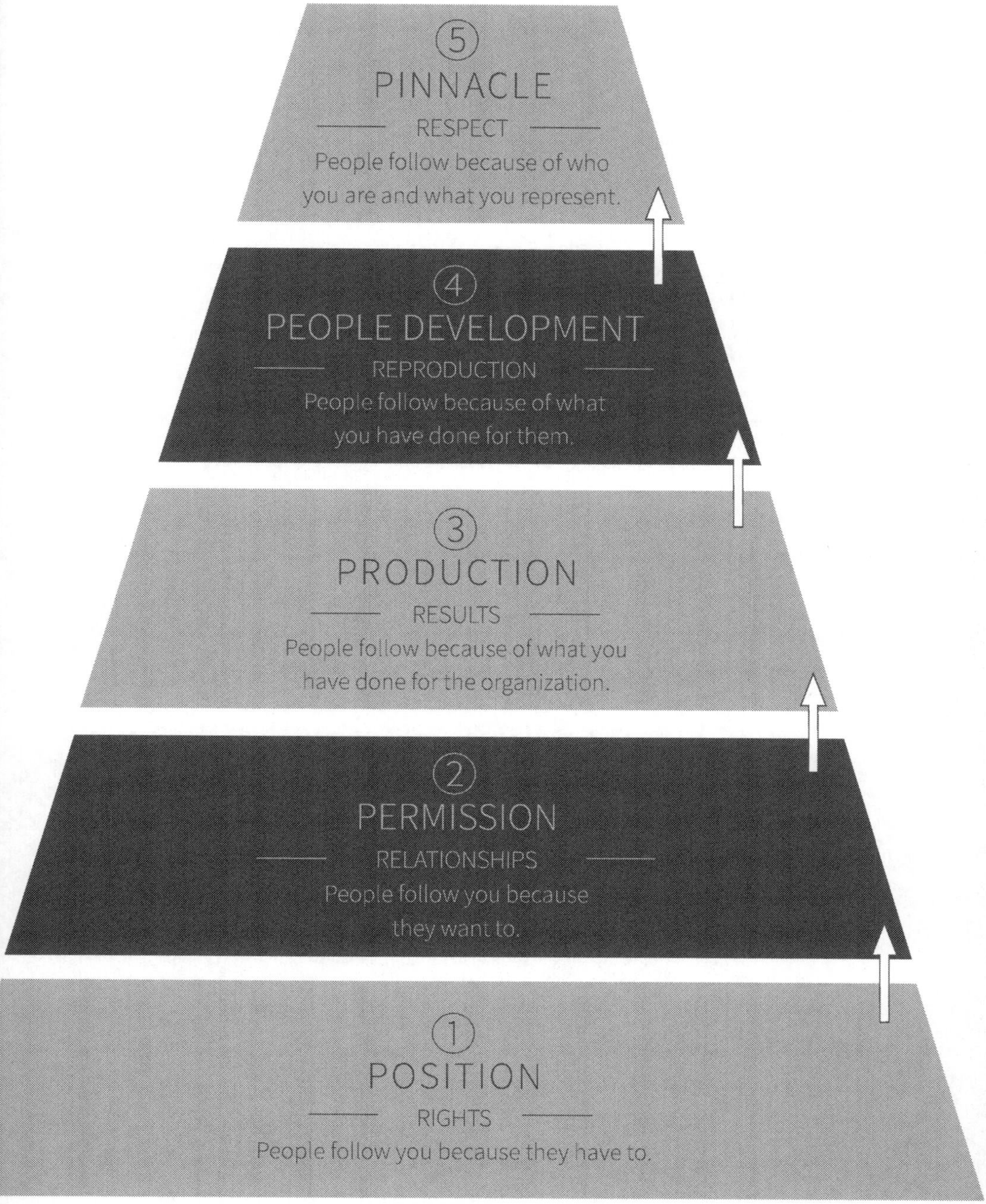

⑤

PINNACLE

RESPECT

People follow because of who
you are and what you represent.

④

PEOPLE DEVELOPMENT

REPRODUCTION

People follow because of what
you have done for them.

③

PRODUCTION

RESULTS

People follow because of what you
have done for the organization.

②

PERMISSION

RELATIONSHIPS

People follow you because
they want to.

①

POSITION

RIGHTS

People follow you because they have to.

#change

CHAPTER 17

Change - Equip Your Team

In the Gallup study of engagement, one of the most basic needs for a team member is cited as the necessary resources to do their jobs.

The data also strongly indicates that the level of engagement of team members has a significant impact on the perception of whether the team member felt they were equipped and had the tools and resources they needed to do their job.

What is fascinating in the study is that the most engaged work groups almost unanimously felt they were well-equipped for the job, whereas those teams that were most disengaged felt they were not appropriately equipped to do their job.

This was apparently true among teams in highly regulated environments, where the provisioning of equipment and resources is very standardized.

The study determined that the leaders and managers who were significantly involved with their teams and proactively attempted to help the team get the resources they needed, created an environment where the team felt heard and their needs were respected.

This directly aligns with the *Affinity Principle*. When leaders immerse themselves in the team experience and put their people first this support is reciprocated by the team.

When we think about equipping our teams, our mind usually goes to the tangibles such as physical tools, equipment, and resources we need to do our work. Obviously, these are incredibly important and vital resources to do our work.

However, many of the soft skills, training, and emotional resources we help our team acquire under our stewardship are equally important in equipping those team members to do their very best in the workplace.

Change Management

An example of this is Change Management. Most modern organizations are dealing with escalating rates of change. Pivots are seemingly more the norm than the exception these days.

Equipping yourself and your team to manage change is one way we can make our team members and organization more successful and resilient.

The inevitability of change is a given, and as a leader and a manager, it is equally inevitable that you'll be involved in managing change throughout your career. It could be as simple as how you manage change in certain aspects of your day-to-day operations, or it may be as complex as managing a huge organizational pivot, or massive policy change.

In managing change, we need to understand that most systems seek homeostasis, and yet rarely achieve that state of equilibrium they seek for very long. Our goal in equipping our teams for change is to regain stability of the interdependent elements impacted by the change with the minimum disruption as quickly as possible. This movement to restore stability and equilibrium can mean the difference between projects succeeding, stalling, or failing.

When you are aware of how you manage change and your related skill sets, it helps you manage elements that impact your peers, your team, and your customers and maintain Affinity.

Understanding that when change happens, people naturally go through a variety of stages which can range from shock and denial at the initial point of disruption to acceptance and commitment at the end. When we manage and equip our teams for change, the incidence of negative consequences is reduced and the time to adjust is reduced substantially.

One common belief is that people resist change on principle, and I've rarely found this to be the case. More often, there is perceived associated discomfort and fear around the unknown or need to learn something new.

People develop expertise and routines over time and when we upend that for them, even for all the right reasons, we create stress.

It is incumbent on us as leaders to use empathy when implementing change and ideally give people time to build new skills or acclimate themselves to the potential changes in advance.

Change *managed* over time can significantly reduce negative consequences as the change curve on the next page illustrates.

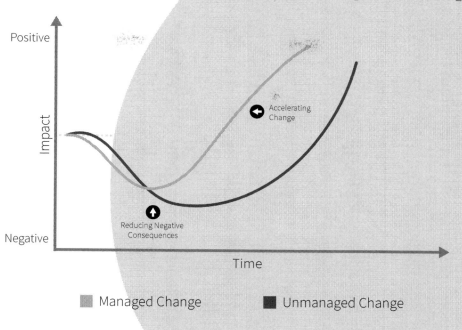

Similarly to when you are working with someone that processes internally and needs time to contemplate, it makes sense to provide the information about the impending change as far in advance as possible.

Of critical importance is elucidating the *why* of the change that is planned.

It also makes sense to provide information in bite-size chunks, so team members can assimilate the information and have time to process. With this incremental approach, hopefully they'll begin to understand what is happening and start to think about how they can help.

Communication is critical in every stage, but when you're equipping your team for change, you need to communicate really well.

As I've discussed previously, communication is a two-way street, so mechanisms that allow team members to ask questions should always be provided and readily available.

As people begin to assimilate the information and ask questions, you may get active or passive resistance to the impending change. Hopefully, you will have anticipated the impacts the change will have and the objections team members might make.

Empathy is key here and your communications need to be clear and supportive.

You may get some unanticipated push-back and keeping your ears and eyes open throughout this transition phase is essential.

As acceptance and exploration of the change develop, training and acclimation should continue, and you need to remain vigilant for issues or resistance that have not run their course.

Time is key and if you've allowed enough lead time people will have the time they need to adapt.

As the change starts to set in and team members begin to find their new rhythm, and hopefully feel the positive impact of the change, production and efficiency should be rising and you'll start seeing the benefits.

Celebrating the success and the positive outcome will help underwrite the next change element you need to present. If you have Affinity and you've been a great steward throughout this transition, the next major change process should be even easier.

Mindful Change Management in Action

One of my consulting clients, Rebecca, went through a massive change prior to me working with her. When she described the transition, which meant laying off an entire division and almost 40% of her workforce, it became evident to me that Rebecca had handled this change really well, even though it took a huge emotional toll on her.

Rebecca had managed the change with great communication and empathy. She created as much lead time as possible and really conveyed the why's and how's very clearly to her team. She met in groups and one-on-one with team members who were being released and actively pursued leads to place people wherever she could. In fact, that was when I first met Rebecca in a CEO Forum and she was canvassing the CEO group for opportunities for people she had to lay off.

Importantly, Rebecca also met with team members who were staying on. She focused on equipping her remaining team to move forward in the face of monumental change and a huge setback. The fact that she kept her company on course and maintained Affinity with her team was a testament to how well she equipped her team in advance and during this transition.

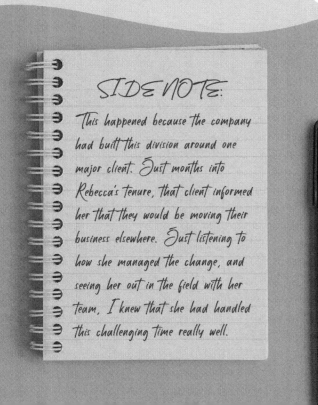

SIDE NOTE:

This happened because the company had built this division around one major client. Just months into Rebecca's tenure, that client informed her that they would be moving their business elsewhere. Just listening to how she managed the change, and seeing her out in the field with her team, I knew that she had handled this challenging time really well.

When it comes to change, emotionally empowering leaders like Rebecca don't just manage the operational aspects of equipping their teams for change. They also help equip their teams for resilience and growth.

The empathy we display and appropriate accommodations we make empower our teams and bring leadership attributes out in team members themselves.

I got to meet several of Rebecca's senior team members and hear their versions of Rebecca's leadership during this tumultuous time. These guys were tough, experienced, and hard to impress. They were highly complimentary of her efforts, her resilience, and they each spoke to the empathy she imparted throughout this process.

These kinds of moments in a company's history are defining. Equipping your team for these huge pivots takes an enormous amount of effort and resilience, but done well you can maintain Affinity and springboard off a tragedy onto great things.

#mentor

CHAPTER 18

Mentor - Grow Your People

men·tor
noun

1. an experienced and trusted adviser

verb

2. advise or train (someone, especially a younger colleague)

John Maxwell describes *Level 4 Leadership* as "People Development." He says that when you're a Level 4 leader,

"People follow you because of what you have done for them."

He then describes *Level 5 Leadership* as the "Pinnacle of Leadership," which is where,

"People follow you because of who you are and what you represent."

In both these cases, these leaders are Mentors.

A mentor can help develop leaders. In turn, this can inspire those new leaders to perpetuate the cycle of leadership growth, by growing leaders themselves.

What Maxwell would describe as a Level 5 Organization comes from this perpetuation of leadership growth.

As we mature as leaders, our approach to leadership evolves. What I like about Maxwell's model of leadership (pictured previously) is that there are clear increments in leadership development.

I have reviewed this model many times to get a gut check on where I think I am on the continuum with various team members. The thing that has become patently clear is that we will hold differing positions with different team members based on the relationship that we have developed. In other words, I may be a Level 4 Leader with one team member in a company, and a Level 2 Leader with another.

Having said that, as you climb the steps of Leadership, I have found that people that you have impacted positively, that have come to trust you and your leadership, people who see you in the upper echelon of this pyramid, take it upon themselves to positively influence others.

For example, when a new team member comes on, it is natural for them to feel out the leadership and be influenced by their peers and supervisors. If that supervisor is a good leader and they have a high opinion of you as a leader, that supervisor will positively influence the new team member's opinion as it forms. If the supervisor is not a good leader, yet they see you in a very positive light, their ability to influence the new team member is diminished.

My point is that influence spreads. Both positive influence and negative influence.

If as a leader and a mentor you invest time and effort into your team, what you share will flow through the entire organization. If you allow your influence to spread organically, it will take a lot of time for that influence to take root. You can be a great Level 2 or Level 3 Leader, but until you start directly and intentionally influencing your nascent leaders you can't move to Level 4 or beyond.

You don't have to subscribe to Maxwell's Model of Leadership to agree with the premise that the greatest leaders are those that grow leaders and encourage leaders to grow others.

This premise is well recognized throughout leadership history and literature.

Equally, as we seek leadership excellence, we need mentors. Throughout my career, I have had some amazing mentors but I have also missed out on opportunities to learn more from some. I am innately very independent and when I look back, I feel I could have gleaned more wisdom from some of the potential mentors that came into my life.

Today, I more clearly recognize the need to actively seek opportunities to mentor and to attract mentors, especially in the areas where I need and seek growth. This realization has demanded a more intentional approach, especially to seek out mentors. The primary reason I need to actively seek to attract mentors is that I am not naturally wired that way. This has become apparent as I have proactively sought to expand my self-awareness.

So, as much as I encourage you to seek opportunities to mentor, I equally challenge you to actively seek mentors for yourself.

No matter where you are on your journey, there's likely a willing mentor who has been in a similar position to you at this point in your career who could offer very real value to your journey.

Much like buying and reading a book, I see a mentor as a resource that has specific learnings to impart. The very fact that you're reading this book suggests that you are open to these opportunities to learn.

So whether you are seeking a mentor, or have a mentoring opportunity here are some thoughts on what a mentor might provide and receive.

Mentors can provide a resource to bounce ideas off. Having an experienced person provide feedback on ideas and initiatives you are planning can shortcut the process and help avoid inconspicuous traps.

A mentor can also offer accountability.

Sometimes, we need someone to whom we make an account. On several occasions, I have been involved in companies or projects where a savvy investor can be both a great mentor and a resource to provide accountability. In these cases, there's an obvious mutually beneficial synergy here.

A mentor can also provide support, especially during tough times. It often feels like you're alone at the top and when things unravel, it's incredibly helpful to have an experienced resource to talk through things with.

To finish this thought on finding mentors for yourself, it is important to find people who really have wisdom and real-world applicability to offer. Do your research and ensure that the mentor has substance. As a consultant, I have acted as a paid mentor to many companies, and have abdicated this opportunity on occasion where I didn't feel I had the requisite experience.

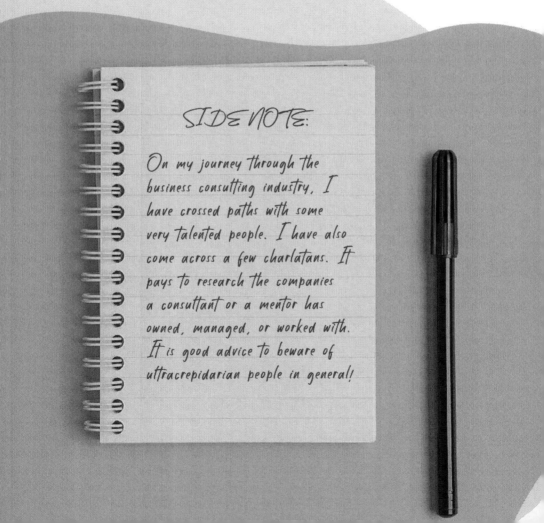

SIDE NOTE:

On my journey through the business consulting industry, I have crossed paths with some very talented people. I have also come across a few charlatans. It pays to research the companies a consultant or a mentor has owned, managed, or worked with. It is good advice to beware of ultracrepidarian people in general!

ul·tra·crep·i·dar·i·an
noun

1. a person who criticizes, judges, or gives advice outside the area of his or her expertise

Just like hiring a new team member, we want to make great decisions for the long haul and doing an appropriate amount of due diligence on the front end can save a lot of pain down the road with a mentor or consultant who is operating outside their area of expertise.

Similarly, as a mentor, we need to be intentional about who we mentor and be judicious with the allocation of our time and energy. We should ensure firstly that we believe we can add value to the situation. We also need to ascertain that the recipient of our advice and experience is open to feedback. There is no prerequisite that they must take your advice, but I have found on occasion that ego gets in the way and it can be a very frustrating and fruitless exercise for both parties.

I haven't spoken a lot about ego in this book, but I do feel that an unhealthy ego is the greatest hubris to leadership and Affinity.

Confidence is really important and positive self-worth builds confidence, but an overabundant ego can distort confidence, and in turn perspective, and ultimately negatively impact one's ability to be an effective leader and mentor.

I have seen leaders I have worked with struggle with ego and in some cases fail to bring their brilliance to bear in a mentorship role because of their overinflated ego.

Sometimes, this is a function of an overly inflated opinion of oneself, but often it is as simple as a lack of self-awareness.

Know What You Don't Know

One of my mentors, Phil, who has been an incredibly successful business-man, routinely says:

"Know what you don't know."

That quote is a great piece of mentorship in and of itself. Just that one line repeated enough, in enough settings, to resonate.

I know that Phil was directing that comment toward me at various times to get me to focus and bring my awareness to my actions. It took some tough lessons, combined with that simple piece of advice, to shift my thinking in regard to where I should focus my energy.

We need to try and put our ego away when it comes to mentoring and that means both parties. That can tend to be difficult at times.

I mentioned that I am very independent. I am also typically unafraid to try new things, or try and fix something which I know very little about. Part of this is my thirst for knowledge and learning. Another part of this is my desire to solve puzzles and come up with solutions. This is confidence bred from pulling things apart and putting them back together and rinsing and repeating enough times that eventually I could get it to work.

In large measure, my propensity to try and be everything to everybody originated from necessity. Much of what I have done, certainly in my early career, was bootstrapping. When you're bootstrapping, you typically need to be a *Jack Of All Trades*. The downside of that is the second part of that adage: *And Master Of None*.

Phil's point that began to resonate with me was that even though I had the confidence to take on almost any challenge or task within the organization, I needed to focus. I also needed to trust in those around me, attract the talent that complemented my skill sets, and grow team members so that in the end they could do that task better than I could because they were focusing or because they had more innate gifts in that area.

As I got better at attracting the right talent, growing team members, and divesting responsibility, the organizations I was working in blossomed and Affinity grew.

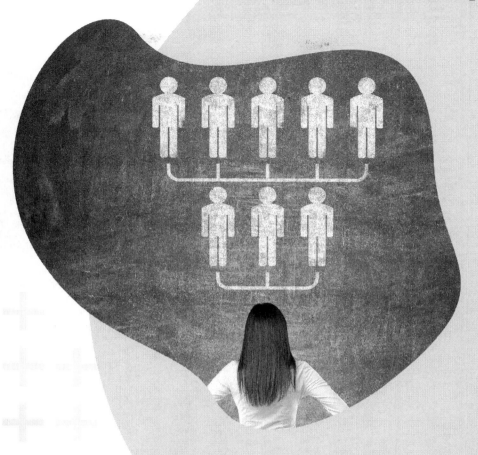

I had to learn to realize where I added most value and let go of things where it was not the best use of my time.

Sometimes things weren't done as well as I may have liked, or exactly the way I would have done them myself, but the organization became scalable.

This lesson also pushed me to be a mentor and to grow team members, and the delight of seeing team members complement, enhance and ultimately surpass my own achievements, was honestly far more rewarding than trying to do everything myself.

Mindful Mentorship in Action

An example of mindful mentorship in my career was a young man I hired in the early years of building Phil's second major business venture, over two decades ago. He was fresh out of college, had good work experience, and a great work ethic. His desire to succeed and grow was unbounded.

Dan exhibited humility and confidence, he was not afraid of getting his hands dirty and had a passion for the fitness industry that we were trying to reshape. He was a lot like me, without the experience. Because he was on a similar track and had similar desires, there was a lot I could offer him initially as a mentor.

Dan became my Assistant General Manager in the first Wellness Center that we had built and as he grew personally and became more experienced, he ultimately became the General Manager. I functioned as his primary mentor and I gained confidence in his abilities over time as he exacted the service and cultural vision that we had defined for this brand.

I worked really closely with Dan and slowly handed off the reins. We would talk regularly and had built a friendship that endures to this day. I was his primary mentor in those early days and when I look back, I feel proud of many of the things we shared, and I learned from him as well.

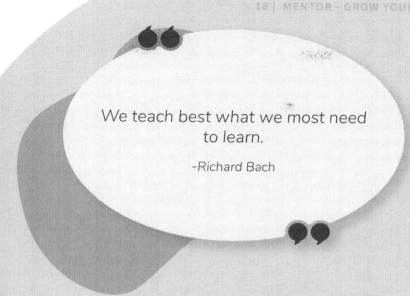

> We teach best what we most need to learn.
>
> -Richard Bach

Almost equally, I look back with disappointment at the things I imparted that did not help Dan, and the things I didn't impart that I should have. This is how it goes with mentorship, from my experience.

We tend to learn as much from our mentees as they learn from us.

On some levels, they become a reflection of us, and in some cases amplify areas we need to work on ourselves.

My point is that mentorship is an organic experience. As much as we need to approach it with intentionality, mentorship will deliver unintended lessons to us as mentors that we need to learn often as frequently as it delivers lessons to the mentee.

Dan progressed in the organization and we decided to send him off to head up our new flagship, V2.0 of the wellness model. A brand new 120,000 s.f. club that sat on 20+ acres in West Chester, Pennsylvania. It was a tough gig building Affinity from the ground up in that club, but he threw his heart and soul into it.

My mentorship of Dan became more spasmodic as we were separated by a 5-hour drive and we were both incredibly busy. Over time, Dan's entrepreneurial juices started to percolate to the surface, and he left the company some years later.

Today, Dan owns a very successful contracting business and even though we're both really busy we catch up every so often and I marvel at the successful businessman he has become.

The next large wellness center we did was in Richmond, VA. This time, rather than sending one person to recreate the culture, we selected multiple talented and transferable team members who could fill out the next club almost immediately. We had begun to create a farm team system that significantly deepened our pool of talent and allowed us to transfer multiple people at a time without losing momentum at the source.

This allowed us to implant our culture and significantly shorten the lead time to Affinity, and ultimately profitability.

I do believe mentoring is a very necessary part of a leader's ascension. It is also a critical piece of an organization that seeks Affinity. The very essence of sharing and giving in this form builds trust, integration, and performance.

Intentional mentoring better equips your team for what lies ahead and helps raise your team up.

This, in turn, helps unleash their innate gifts. It also shows how much you care.

In essence, mentoring exemplifies many elements of this book.

Maxwell says that becoming a Level 4 Leader takes time and an immense amount of focus, energy, and skill.

However, becoming a Level 5 Leader demands many innate gifts.

This pinnacle in Maxwell's treatise may be unattainable to some, but you can choose to stare at that peak with longing eyes, or you can take the first step toward it, and then follow it with another. Before you know it, you just might be looking down from what appeared to be a completely unattainable position, marveling at the gifts you uncovered on the journey.

#community

CHAPTER 19

Community - Nurture Affinity & Team Integration

com·mu·ni·ty
noun

1. a group of people living (or working) in the same place or having a particular characteristic in common

2. a feeling of fellowship with others, as a result of sharing common attitudes, interests, and goals

There are fundamentals in the creation and nurturing of a culture of community and Affinity within an organization, and I have discussed many of these elements in previous chapters.

A vision is a powerful focal point for teams.

When your team shares a vision, it is much easier to gain cohesion and a more organizational orientation, versus a departmental orientation.

Interdepartmental turf wars are routine in growing companies, often because there is a lack of shared vision. These turf wars usually start as a function of conflict in the leadership team and this siloing effect dramatically impacts a company's ability to function optimally and build community.

The team looks to its leaders to recognize this compartmentalization and rebuild community, and ultimately create Affinity, between departments and within the company as a whole.

More than anyone, the leadership team needs to share the overarching vision and that is not always easy when you have strong-minded and driven people leading departments, divisions, and the company.

It can sometimes feel as if we are at cross purposes within an organization, and when we are at odds we isolate and insulate our teams and create silos.

This might feel like a natural position to take, but unless we look at the organization as a whole, we will start to wobble.

Reinforcing Common Goals

I headed up a company that had a number of sales channels. Each of these channels had a channel manager, and inadvertently there were times when we had a conflict between these channels. These conflicts came up in terms of commissions, territory, overlap and resource distribution.

There were heated discussions between the various parties and I often had to adjudicate and arbitrate these discussions. Sometimes, I had even created the tension, with a decision that I had backed. At all times, I would try and bring our focus back to the end goal and layer in the various channel contributions.

I would routinely point out how each channel contributed and how when one channel was slow, another channel would often help offset that softening. One phenomenon we saw across these channels was between Amazon and our on-line retail. As Amazon grew, our own on-line sales typically diminished. As I have stated earlier in the book, Amazon taking on-line business from us meant that we were relinquishing *ownership of the customer* and that was a problem.

Our strategic decisions to put a governor on Amazon didn't feel great for the Amazon channel, but there were bigger things at stake. We knew that if we took the emphasis off of Amazon from a marketing standpoint and put our resources into our own retail sales, we would see a shift in that direction.

These kinds of decisions could easily create dissension and discord between departments. I was really cognizant of reinforcing the common goal we had to drive overall revenue and to ideally create Affinity with *our* customers. Conveying these underlying drivers was essential.

It is never easy to keep the focus on larger company goals when departmental objectives are compromised, but it is critical.

It is our job as leaders to keep our focus on the big picture and draw the individual team's focus out to that horizon when necessary.

What you are doing as the leader is recognizing the interconnectedness of departments, and divisions of a company, and distilling them into a unified focus to encourage collaboration, teamwork and the achievement of the shared goal. Building community across departments helps underwrite these efforts.

Interdisciplinary Collaboration

Dr. Ralph Cohen, a very good friend and mentor of mine who passed away in 2016, was a champion for interdisciplinary collaboration. In 2013, at age 96, Ralph established the Cohen Center for the Study of Technological Humanism at James Madison University in Virginia.

The feat of establishing an interdisciplinary center as a nonagenarian (a person in their nineties) in and of itself is amazing. To me, the innovative foundations and thought leadership of this center were even more extraordinary.

Ralph, who had retired as William R. Kenan Jr. Professor Emeritus of English at the University of Virginia in 2009, after a tenure of 42 years, had a vision of an interdisciplinary graduate education that created community between normally disparate faculties.

By establishing the Cohen Center for the Humanities, Ralph was championing interdisciplinary discussions from which topics of mutual interest would emerge. He was also providing forums and resources for graduate students to engage in intellectual exchanges. Much of his premise for this center was to provide opportunities for graduate students to broaden their viewpoints and better direct their intellectual and professional development.

Ralph postulated, for example, that discourse between the arts community and the engineering and science disciplines could benefit each of these typically siloed faculties. Ralph and I discussed this at length as it related to business and the cross-departmental benefits of building a community within an organization.

What Ralph was championing was a sense of community through communication and exploration. He was breaking down walls that restricted the flow of ideas, experiences, backgrounds, and shared knowledge.

He used common issues and concerns, shared through events and activities, and that engaged a cross-section of faculties in formal and informal settings and discussions.

If we follow this model within our businesses, I believe the cross-pollination will not only enhance community, but it will also improve outcomes for the various departments and divisions.

In understanding each other, and the challenges we face, our empathy grows, and Affinity is fostered.

Launch

In this vein of cross-pollination and community creation, one of the basics I have implemented in every organization I have managed over the years is the new team member orientation. A good friend of mine, Tim Rhode, from the Rhode Management Company, coined the term Launch for this orientation. I love that name and have used it myself in a variety of settings.

What we do when we properly orient a new team member is to launch them into the community, and hopefully onto success within your organization.

Fundamental to the *Launch* is the new team member spending time in each and every department. That does not mean a nickel tour, or a drive-by, it means the team member actually working in that department for an hour, half a day, or even a day.

Our level of understanding and empathy for our fellow team members increases exponentially when we have walked in their shoes, even if only for a brief period of time.

Extend this concept to a regular rotation across departments.

Cross-Pollination

A great example of this happened in a weekly All-Team meeting I was running. Our head of Customer Service was pointing out that Customer Service would be down for an hour once a week while that team had a departmental team meeting. Andrew, the Chief Technology Officer for the company volunteered his team, on the spot, to cover the phones for that hour.

It would be easy for the IT team to have concerns moving so far out of their normal scope of operations. Equally, you could imagine the Customer Service team being concerned handing the phones, chats and email responses over to a third party, let alone the IT nerds.

This is where this anecdote beautifully reflects the power of community and Affinity. The head of Customer Service, Teppi, and the head of IT, Andrew, had worked with me in a previous company and had both come to join me in this new venture. They trusted each other, had Affinity with each other, and intrinsically knew the benefits of this cross-pollination.

Affinity also ran deep between these teams and when this idea was presented to each team, it was quickly embraced.

The upshot of this was a logical progression of synergy between these two teams. After only a few weeks on the phones and Customer Service platform, the IT team had a much better appreciation of the many challenges (technical and otherwise) the customer service team faced and began chipping away, where they could, at these challenges . . . because they were experiencing them first-hand.

This is a pointed example, but one that underlines everything I am promoting in this chapter, and throughout this book.

When we support each other across our organization, empathy and camaraderie grow. Affinity builds with a growing appreciation of the challenges we each face in doing our jobs. To any extent that we can illuminate those challenges across departments, a more unified approach will synthesize into amplified achievements for the entire organization.

Ralph's Technological Humanism

This example of technology meeting humanism and amplifying performance would have resonated with Ralph. This was another major tenet of his, where he saw the interconnectedness of knowledge and the intersection of *technology and humanism*.

The other defining achievement for Ralph, and his wife Libby, was the vast community of colleagues and former students they had developed internationally over some 70 years. These relationships with leading scholars and thought leaders from every discipline proved invaluable to the Cohen Center and their academic community. As a function of Ralph and Libby's immense *community*, the JMU Cohen Center of the Center for the Humanities has attracted many distinguished guests and academics and became a hub of engagement and Affinity for graduate students.

Ralph & Libby's Community

Ralph's wife, Libby Okun Cohen, was renowned for creating community wherever she went. I first met Ralph and Libby at a wellness center that was under my leadership, and she was not a happy camper. A salesperson had told Libby one thing and then changed the story in a subsequent discussion. Libby was not one to accept this kind of behavior and I was brought in to resolve the issue. It didn't take long to determine that Libby had good cause to question our integrity and I summarily determined that we should do what we said we would in the first place. This was the beginning of a wonderful friendship that lasted through to Libby's passing in 2013.

Libby and Ralph became communal elders at that particular facility, all the way through to Libby's dramatic decline in health almost a dozen years later.

Much like Ralph, what I loved about Libby was her willingness to challenge convention.

I also loved her strong, outspoken, and inquisitive nature and in that regard, she was very different from Ralph. Rather than her tough outward disposition polarizing people, Libby had this uncanny ability to bring people together through her unequivocal and irreverent nature. In large part, this worked because Libby's underlying good intent was evident.

Libby originally went to graduate school to become a librarian and went on to apply her great love of books and all things literary (possibly in part why she loved Ralph so much) throughout the communities she touched. Imagine the surprise and delight our kids had when they entered the Libby O. Cohen Library at Tandem Friends School in Charlottesville, VA and saw Libby's photo on the wall of the library that was named after her.

Under her inspired and challenging guidance, the multifaceted librarian spearheaded monthly cultural events, inventive programs, and outside speakers and generated unprecedented dialogue. The library itself quickly became known as "Tandem's cultural center."

Our kids had grown up around Ralph and Libby and were welcomed as part of their community. They would listen to their opinions and share their wisdom with them. Their openness was quite amazing.

Ralph and Libby listened, they joined hands with others, they broke bread, encouraged discourse, they sought diversity, and they believed in joining communities together to be one.

Ralph and Libby's contributions to community continue today in many realms, including the Cohen Center, where the Libby Okun Cohen Chair in technological humanism perpetuates her memory. And Ralph's belief in interdisciplinary education is building foundations for future leaders to look at their organizations in a more communal way.

Integrating Parts into a Whole

As we come to understand how the various parts of the whole complement each other and intertwine, we can further enhance Affinity and team integration.

In recognizing these interrelationships, we also need to recognize that motivating team members to synergize takes a variety of strategies and tactics.

Tactics can include individual and team incentives. These can come in many forms such as shared voice, encouragement, and investing in team members' growth. These more intangible forms of motivation have in my experience far more lasting impact than financial incentives.

Having said that, for some team members financial incentives will trump the less tangible forms of motivation.

Understanding what incentives work for individuals and teams will help you tactically and strategically reduce the incidence of "it's not my problem" and "us and them" responses from teams and individuals.

Communication Preferences

How we communicate with team members also needs to vary. At one point, earlier on in my career, I got a little frustrated that one of my departments in a company I was leading; they were seemingly ignoring email updates I'd been sending out. As it turned out, most of the people in that department didn't even have computers. As a result I started dropping into this department when they were taking a break and would download the latest news and information verbally. This instantly resolved the problem and taught me a valuable lesson.

Even today, how you communicate with your team members and teams at large needs to account for preferences. Communications can vary broadly from in-person meetings all the way to All-Team events. Some people are more responsive to text messages, versus emails. Some read the notices on the break room noticeboard. Regardless, it makes sense to communicate in as many forms as possible if you want to engage as many of your team members as possible in the execution of your tactics and strategies.

Mindful Communication in Action

Equally important to team integration and the quest for Affinity is feedback.

I was meeting with some clients and they were describing the dysfunction that was occurring in their team with miscommunications. They were thinking that they needed to get a weekly newsletter going to stamp out the rumors and misunderstandings that were arising as they integrated a new business into their existing operations.

I suggested that a newsletter is great, but that is ostensibly a monologue and it struck me that what they really needed was to stimulate dialogue. They needed the team to be able to ask questions and give feedback in a safe forum, making it a two-way exchange.

Their challenge was that they had team members working across a broad spectrum of hours and getting them all together was almost impossible, without putting some team members out and marginalizing others. A meeting seemed out of the question, so I suggested a phone or video call.

They didn't have a huge team, so I suggested following the Verne Harnish model of the *Stand-Up* I described earlier in this book. To refresh, this is where each team member gets 60 seconds to inform the rest of the team on how their workweek had gone, what their plan for the following week was. They also got the opportunity to expose any rocks they had in their shoes (challenges they faced). I suggested they also encourage questions that team members might have about what's going on in the business.

The advantage of this (with 15 people on the entire team), appropriately managed, the meeting would be over in 15 minutes. And it created *dialogue*.

They loved this idea and set about implementing this routine for their team. In short order, a lot of the confusion diminished, and dialogue flourished.

Format & Prioritization of Mindful Communication

▶▶ In Person is optimal in many ways. It allows for a full flow of information verbally, visually, auditorily, emotionally and energetically. And in terms of reciprocal value, I would tier the value from these exchanges in the following descending order:

    a. Interpersonal Dialogue
    b. Small-Group Dialogue
    c. Large Group - More Limited Dialogue

▶▶ Video Calls still offer verbal, visual and auditory elements. The emotional and energetic exchange is dampened in this digital forum. I would tier the value of video calls similarly in descending order:

    a. Interpersonal Dialogue
    b. Small-Group Dialogue
    c. Large Group - More Limited Dialogue

▶▶ Phone Calls still offer verbal and auditory elements, with emotional and energetic elements further dulled. I would tier the value of phone calls in this descending order:

    a. Interpersonal Dialogue
    b. Small-Group Dialogue
    c. Large Group - More Limited Dialogue

▶▶ Email or Text offers a communication exchange. Emotions can be evident but misconstrued or misinterpreted more easily. This is a great medium for communications to large groups, in multiple time zones, as it doesn't need to be managed in real-time. It also puts things 'on the record'. When using this forum, I still believe optimal value can generally be achieved with one-on-one interactions following a similar descending order to the other communications methods:

    a. Interpersonal Exchange
    b. Team Exchange
    c. All-Team

Creating Meaningful Connections

While managing a team of managers across a large region in the US, I inherited a weekly video call. On this call, it seemed most of the managers would turn their video off, which made me question the value of this forum versus a phone call.

This was in the days before video calls had become ubiquitous, and the company had spent a lot of money on hardware and software to support this forum.

Turns out, most of the managers felt the call was a complete waste of time and that they had better things to do like emails or reports. So they logged into the call and simply turned their video and microphone off. They worked away in the background and let the leaders drone on while they got their work done. In this way, they were marked present but very definitely were not present.

I personally understood the intended value of the meeting but apparently, these meetings had been inordinately long and were mainly about reviewing numbers and sales targets. I felt that there were other ways to monitor and manage to the numbers. I felt strongly that the real value of this call was in connecting, sharing, communicating and exploring.

So the premise of the meeting changed. Maximum of 30 minutes; all video feeds and microphones on; everyone was expected to contribute to the dialogue; and, the goal was to share best practices and to walk away with at least one tangible we could each focus on for the next week and report back on at the following meeting.

It took a while to get everyone present for the call and to get a rhythm going, but over the course of a month or so, we started to really get value from the exchange. It wasn't the same as meeting in person, but otherwise these managers only saw each other every twelve months at the Annual Strategic Planning Retreat, so getting this enhanced level of exchange and sharing best practices definitely helped build camaraderie among this geographically separated group.

Regardless of the size of your organization, implementing cross-departmental communications and initiatives, encouraging feedback from inside and outside of departments, and creating communication rhythms, will obviate the need for long meetings and encourage interaction between team members at all levels.

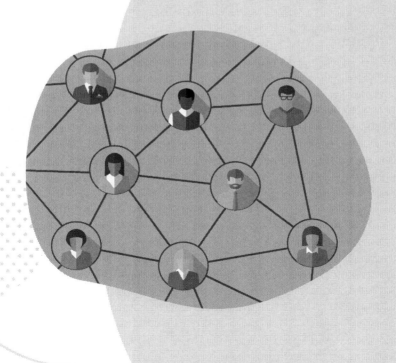

Ultimately, we need to create connections between teams and team members. We need to facilitate rhythms of engagement and cross-pollination.

This includes encouraging reciprocity and diversity, sharing general and specific knowledge, and fostering meaningful dialogue. All of this is underwritten by the mindful leadership practices I talk about in this book.

AFFINITY THROUGH THE
DEVELOPMENT OF COMMUNITY
& TEAM INTEGRATION

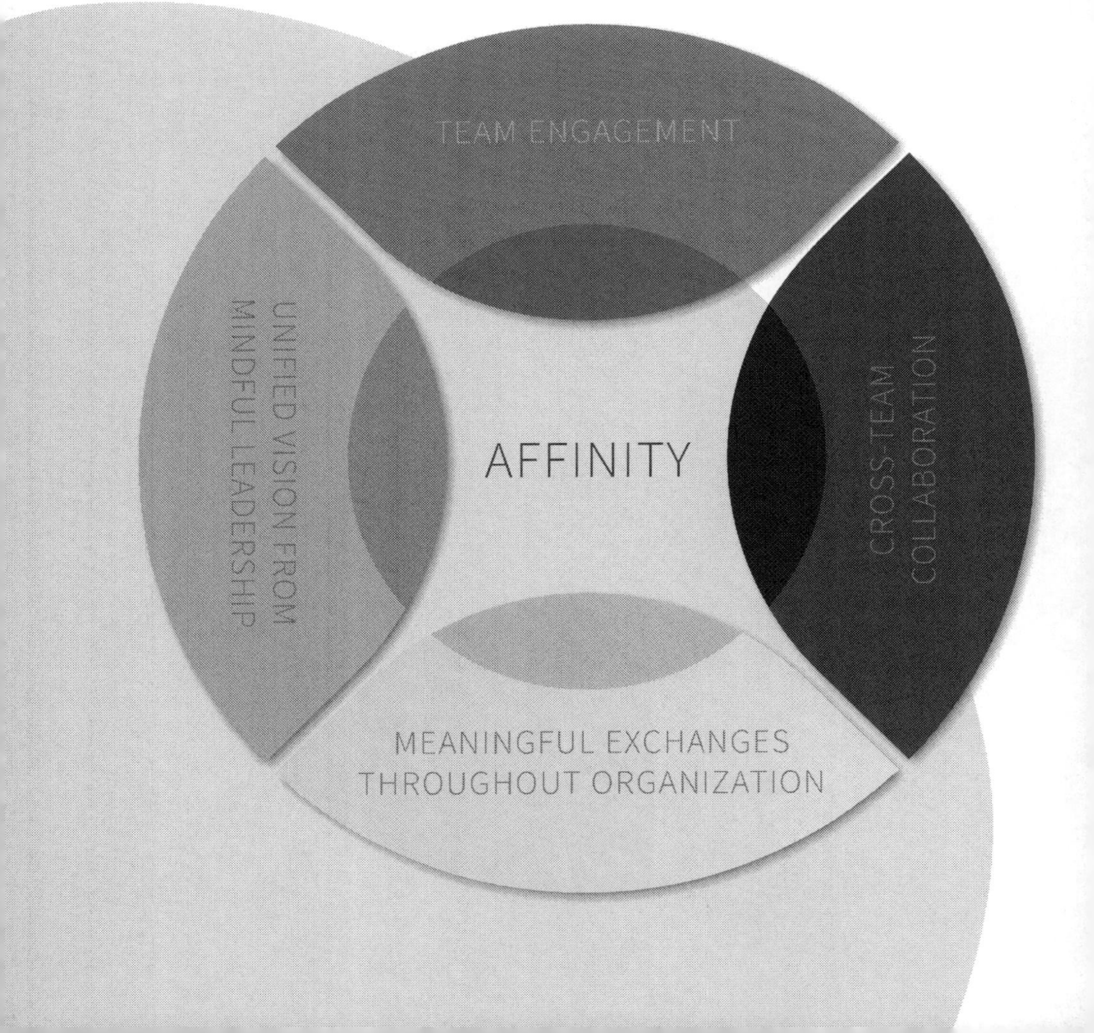

TEAM ENGAGEMENT

UNIFIED VISION FROM
MINDFUL LEADERSHIP

AFFINITY

CROSS-TEAM
COLLABORATION

MEANINGFUL EXCHANGES
THROUGHOUT ORGANIZATION

"True community is based upon equality, mutuality, and reciprocity. It affirms the richness of individual diversity as well as the common human ties that bind us together.
-Pauli Murray"

#bettertogether

#growthmindset

CHAPTER 20

Growth Mindset - Encourage Curiosity & Learning

growth
noun

1. the process of increasing in physical size

mindset
noun

1. the established set of attitudes held by someone

The Growth Mindset is an attitude of prosperity and advancement. It is the 'can do' of high performance teams. When Affinity exists within your team the Growth Mindset follows. Encouragement, curiosity, and learning are all by-products of Affinity.

According to Stanford psychologist Carol Dwecks', "Mindset: The New Psychology of Success," when we have a growth mindset we thrive on challenges and see failures as opportunities. Rather than having a fixed framework of our potential, when we have a growth mindset, we see that framework as a springboard for growing and stretching our existing abilities.

In Dweck's seminal work, she explains that a great deal of our behavior throughout life reflects whether we have adopted a "fixed mindset" or a "growth mindset".

A fixed mindset assumes that our innate gifts of intelligence, creative ability, and character are indeed fixed. That what we have to bring to the table is not likely to change in any meaningful way.

This in turn drives the individual with a fixed mindset to avoid failures and hunger for approval.

Dweck found that the growth mindset fosters a curiosity and passion for learning that was founded on a belief that intellect, creativity, and even less measurable attributes like love and friendship can be nurtured with passion, hard work and practice.

When we have the growth mindset, we see failures and setbacks as learning opportunities. And this in and of itself minimizes self-imposed limitations.

Growth mindset does not, however, mean that you're an eternal optimist. It does mean that your passion for stretching yourself, for sticking with it when things aren't going well, allows you to thrive in the toughest times of your life.

It is well documented that Thomas Edison made over 1,000 unsuccessful attempts while attempting to invent the light bulb. A reporter once asked Edison, "How did it feel to fail 1,000 times?" Edison replied, "I didn't fail 1,000 times. The light bulb was an invention with 1,000 steps."

An inherent attribute of a growth mindset is the belief that you can cultivate your talents and aptitudes through effort.

Working Smarter, Not Harder?

One indelible lesson I have repeatedly referenced since my teen years was a story I saw on TV of an English plasterer who was incredibly successful. He had several beautiful homes, a stable of luxury cars, and lived a wonderful life by material standards.

He put his wealth and success down to the fact that he worked much harder than any other plasterer. He used an oversize mud board to hold the plaster. That allowed him to cover more area, more quickly, and therefore get more work done. He worked longer hours, took on more jobs, and essentially outworked everyone in his industry.

I came from a low to middle-class family where my father was a tradesman and this story of a tradesman being this successful really resonated with me.

I acquired the mentality that no matter what I did if I worked harder than everyone else, I could achieve whatever I wanted.

Work hard I did (insert Yoda's voice here). I worked longer hours, pushed myself harder and harder, and drove myself relentlessly toward that nebulous thing called success.

As introspection has become more a part of my nature, I have delved into the underlying motivation for this relentless drive. Was I simply seeking approval through success, or was I trying to "live deep and suck the marrow out of life?" as Thoreau wrote. Did I indeed have a fixed mindset or a growth mindset?

I choose to believe it was the latter because of two undeniable attributes I possess . . . Attributes that are indicative of the Growth Mindset.

I have a passion for learning, and I am not discouraged by failure.

In fact, I don't actually see myself failing in even the most challenging situations. I do, however, see myself learning valuable lessons in life through failure.

In recent years, I have been learning to channel my work ethic more effectively by working smarter and seeking to metabolize my learnings into constructive action. My wife, Jana, has been a source of reflection and regularly dispenses insights that help me self-actualize. I have sought more balance and harmony through those insights and hard-earned lessons, and hopefully this is further reflected in the enhanced quality of my relationships with friends, associates and my family.

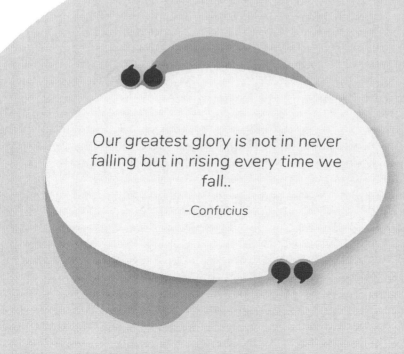

Our greatest glory is not in never falling but in rising every time we fall..

-Confucius

If you are doing some introspection yourself and not liking the conclusions you're coming to, the good news, according to Dweck, is that . . .

we can rewire our cognitive habits to adopt the much more abundant and nourishing growth mindset. And we can also help instill it in others.

That is an essential thread in this chapter: How do we select team members who have a growth mindset, and how do we encourage this abundance mentality in team members we already employ?

On the opposite page is a graphic adapted from Carol Dweck's book, "Mindset: The New Psychology of Success" describing this dichotomy of mindset. This is a simple distillation of this powerful set of insights.

If we use this model to shape questions we would use during an interview process, we can get a sense of whether the candidate in front of us has a *growth mindset* or a *fixed mindset*.

TWO MINDSETS
Carol S. Dweck, Ph.D.

FIXED MINDSET
Intelligence is static

GROWTH MINDSET
Intelligence can be developed

Leads to a desire to **look smart** and a tendency to:

Leads to a desire to **learn** and a tendency to:

Avoid challenges ← CHALLENGES → **Embrace** challenges

Give up easily ← OBSTACLES → **Persist** in the face of setbacks

See effort as **fruitless or worse** ← EFFORT → See effort as **the path to mastery**

Ignore useful negative feedback ← CRITICISM → **Learn** from criticism

Feel **threatened** by the success of others ← SUCCESS OF OTHERS → Find **lessons** and **inspiration** in the success of others

As a result, they may **plateau early** and achieve **less than their full potential**.

As a result, they reach **ever-higher levels of achievement**.

All this confirms a **deterministic view of the world**.

All this gives them a **greater sense of free will**.

Dweck's model can help us divine if that potential team member would seek out and embrace challenges; whether they'd persist in the face of setbacks; whether they'd see effort as a path to mastery; and, whether they'd learn from constructive criticism.

If that candidate imbibes all those attributes and finds inspiration and lessons in the success of others, they will reach for higher levels of achievement in your organization.

Even though we can't rely exclusively on one metric, such as mindset, in hiring I would postulate that . . .

Determining whether a candidate has a growth mindset or not ticks an extremely important box in most hiring scenarios.

I had instinctively defined this growth mindset concept as the *Abundance Mentality* in the past. However, this description does not fully encapsulate the breadth and depth of Dweck's remarkably insightful work and research. But the *Abundance Mentality* definitely aligns on some levels with her findings.

When I have had the joy of working with abundant minded people, Affinity flourishes and even the worst days don't feel that bad.

Expanding this desire to attract growth-minded individuals around me really resonates.

Embracing a growth mindset within your organization obviously starts with you.

Attracting team members who are excited about growth, demonstrate curiosity, are willing to face setbacks and continue on, and want to expand their capabilities, will be a reflection of you. And be fundamental to a company's long-term success.

CHAPTER 21

Challenge - Embracing Innovation

chal·lenge
noun

1.   An objection or query as to the truth of something, often with an implicit demand for proof

> If you always do what you've always done, you'll always get what you've always got.
> -Henry Ford

I could not count how many times I've regurgitated this famous Ford quote. While I would argue that Ford was not on many levels a 'Mindful Leader,' he was one of the greatest innovators of the 20th century.

I have subsequently come to believe that this adage is not typically true today, in the modern world of business.

The truth today might better be described this way:

If we continue to do what we've always done, we'll get less and less of what we've gotten before.

We live in a highly competitive, fast moving and fickle business world. We live in a highly competitive, fast-moving, and fickle business world. What is all the rage today can be sidelined overnight and replaced by bigger, better, smaller, taller alternatives.

The life-cycle of a product or a service enjoying significant market share (without making continued and often significant adjustments) is getting shorter and shorter. Competition and commoditization is escalating at unprecedented rates.

Status quo is short-lived in almost any business today.

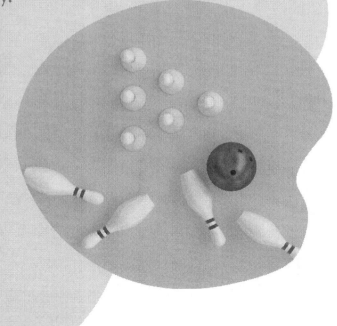

As a result, leaders are continually asked to reevaluate, rethink, retool, re-engineer, and rebirth elements of their products and services, and even their whole companies.

Therefore, *Innovation* must be encouraged within organizations that hope to survive, let alone thrive and create. *Challenging the status quo* is a non-negotiable.

To that end, *Innovation* is an essential lever that increases profitability and growth within organizations.

In a study of over 650 companies, researchers found that the top 25% of innovators within the study had 13% higher profitability than the firms with average innovation strategies. Additionally, startups and new products coming to market had a 30% shorter "time to break even" in the more innovative companies. (Arthur D. Little study, 2013.)

In a controlled study by Dobni (2011), they determined that highly innovative companies had a direct and positive relationship to top line growth, customer satisfaction, bottom line growth, and profitability. Dobni also found that organizations with a low innovation orientation had a direct and significant correlation with poor return on investment, lackluster firm performance, and lowered overall enterprise value.

Fostering innovation within an organization and challenging the status quo starts with leadership.

Yet according to Harvard Business review, 72% of leaders admit that they rarely challenge the status quo within their organizations.

This is bookended by an industry study undertaken by Accenture (2013), which revealed that merely 18% of executives believe their company's innovation efforts deliver a competitive advantage.

Overcoming organizational inertia, challenging the status quo, and championing an innovation strategy is not easy, but substantial research supports the need for leaders to manage strategic innovation in order to ensure ongoing organizational performance.

It should also be considered that we often seek innovation when we have no choice. Examples would be when we're losing market share, or our products or services are being marginalized by factors out of our control. Worse still, redundancy could be staring us down, and often we turn to innovation when it is too late.

Obviously, the best time to innovate is when you are not in a compromised position.

Innovation in Action

I have a colleague from a CEO forum who is the CEO of a large print and digital media company that I have long admired. In recent years, Adam has helped steer this company through innovation after innovation, in an industry that had been beleaguered by closures, consolidations, and on-line commoditization.

Adam reached out to me to do some consulting and during discovery, I sought to understand what he was up against and his motivation for reaching out in the first place.

He explained that they were in a really strong position, pretty much at the top of their game, and he felt that now's the time to capitalize on their position rather than when they were in a downward cycle or a lull in the market.

This underlined aspects of Adam's wiring that highlighted why he had been so successful in growing this company.

He was a fierce competitor and never happy with the status quo. He wanted to innovate and improve when he had the luxury of time and resources.

Adam drove innovation to stay relevant in a highly competitive industry and he always wanted to be ahead of the curve, not playing catch-up.

The other thing we explored during discovery was their on-line presence. Adam had explained that they had bandwidth to significantly increase production capacity. His sales team was doing a good job covering the region and winning business. But as with most businesses, they were besieged by on-line competition.

I suggested that they consider an on-line presence themselves and compete for segments of that marketplace in which they could excel. They had the infrastructure and the bandwidth. They had a great shipping and mailing division and they also a newly acquired digital marketing division that built websites and e-commerce platforms for clients. They had everything they needed to innovate into that space.

Adam's response was what I would have expected: bells going off, wheels turning, and I knew that he would be pursuing this idea diligently to its logical conclusion. I did know that Adam would consider all aspects, seek counsel, meet with his team members and if the opportunity was there to innovate, he would embark upon it with enthusiasm.

Adam and his team have a proud 70+ year history in an industry that has been declared obsolete by many pundits. As he and his team continue to embrace innovation, their company will no doubt prosper into the years to come.

SIDE NOTE:

Adam's company implemented an ESOP (Employee Stock Ownership Plan) many years back and is now over 90% employee owned. This in and of itself is an innovative path for companies to consider.

An ESOP can provide unique rewards for team members, and in turn for the company. Participants in the plan can receive significant retirement benefits at no financial cost to them. Additionally, an ESOP is a great way to enhance the company's ability to recruit and retain top talent. When team members have a stake in their company, it can ignite a mindset that can underwrite innovation and overall enhanced performance. Given all the obvious benefits of including people in the ownership stakes, less than 10% of team members in the U.S. are in an ESOP program.

#esop

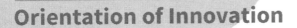

Orientation of Innovation

Many leaders who appreciate the benefits of innovation and embrace the need to challenge the status quo are developing and sustaining an orientation of innovation within their organizations.

This orientation toward innovation needs to be communicated clearly in the company's core values and strategic plan.

This in turn needs to stimulate ongoing conversations to ensure that any innovation aligns with the overall company strategy and isn't just innovation for innovation's sake.

Ready, Fire, Aim

When I was managing a company some years back, our senior executive team agreed that we needed to do a better job encouraging innovation and rewarding innovators. We felt that we were becoming overly bureaucratic and even though checks and balances are necessary as companies mature, we felt innovation was not being actively encouraged, and attempts at innovation were often being stifled by red tape and a *fixed mindset*.

Inherent in this shift in focus was the understanding that sometimes people would break things on the way to creating something innovative.

Therefore, in order to encourage an innovative mindset in our team, we also needed to reward excellent failures and not just celebrate the successes.

This could be achieved by creating an environment where well-motivated mistakes by team members were not punished but welcomed. We needed Affinity, and to create an environment where innovation could flourish.

With Affinity flowing and an environment that welcomed trials and errors, we then wanted to ignite innovation in a very tangible way. To this end, we created the 'Ready, Fire, Aim' Award (as opposed to the usual version 'Ready, Aim Fire').

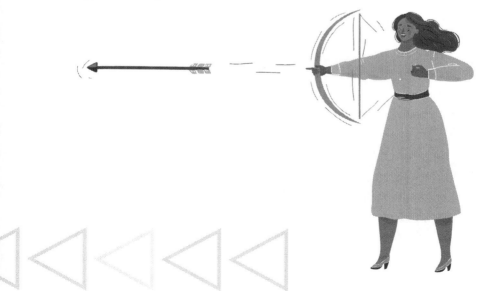

Implicit in this award was the fact that the team member may circumvent some of the usual checks and balances or might try something before fully fleshing out the details, in order to innovate. The award wasn't always based on success. It was equally available for valiant attempts or for resilience in the face of bureaucratic opposition.

This award was made very public and was on offer to any team member. Team members could nominate themselves, they could be recommended by a fellow team member, or the executive team could nominate them.

Regardless, these awards started to catch on.

People would receive $1,500 if they came up with an innovation that could grow company revenue, solve a major problem, save the company money, or in some way contribute to the company innovating and growing.

Even though we annually acknowledged contributors to our Intrinsic Purpose and Core Values, we decided to make the 'Ready, Fire, Aim' Award a quarterly offering. This spurred further engagement from the team and kept the concept front and center for those team members who felt inspired to innovate.

Fostering Innovation in Your Company Culture

If you're intrigued by the idea of enhancing your company's innovative drive, ask yourself what you could do to communicate this, and get team members throughout your organization focused on driving positive change from within.

Importantly, if you feel the innovation within your culture is stilted or non-existent, you need to shift focus toward innovation as a long-term play. Developing effective innovation implementation activities takes time and planning.

You also need to allow for the progression of ideas from the initial concept through to full-scale implementation. Celebrating little victories is tantamount (remember Baby Steps) and reinforces the establishment of an innovative culture.

Support systems and resources need to be put in place in order to create and encourage a process for innovation.

Resources can include financial rewards, mentors, support teams, access to experts or consultants, training programs, and forums.

Of absolute necessity is engaging team members in the innovation process. Wherever possible, draw on internal resources to support initiatives. This seeds buy-in from team members and can potentially lead to innovation from within the company that enhances, complements, or initiates a unique innovation process.

By inviting different perspectives to an innovation project, we are increasing engagement. If departments and team members outside the direct relationship with the innovation drive are aware of the initiative, contributions will come from some very unexpected places.

This demands transparency and means opening up dialogue throughout the organization to nurture new perspectives and seeds of change. In other words, Affinity needs to be flowing through your company's veins.

Champions

For any innovation project, you need a champion.

If the innovation is coming from the top down, I encourage you strongly to find a genuine champion for the project before embarking on the journey. This means someone who is incredibly passionate about the project/concept/idea. If you can't find a true champion, I would rethink embarking on that journey until you find that motivated change agent.

I've made the mistake of appointing a person to a project that wasn't passionate about it. Being a good team member, they'd agree to drive the innovation but didn't necessarily have the drive to make it happen at all costs. This rarely goes as well as you would hope.

When someone wants a project to succeed at all costs, they will champion that project forward.

If they're merely doing it because they've been asked to do it, the chance of them having the drive to overcome the inevitable obstacles of innovation is much lower. This team member will need to launch and grow that innovation project in the face of numerous unforeseen challenges and the chances of them making it happen are far less than when you have a passionate and invested team member championing the cause.

This is why an innovation up strategy is so effective. By default, the champion has nominated themselves for the project and if they're truly passionate about it, they'll drive the project from concept to reality, or bust.

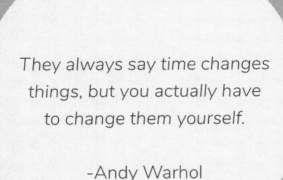

They always say time changes things, but you actually have to change them yourself.

-Andy Warhol

#driveinnovation

Innovation Strategy

When setting out to implement innovation, there are two sides to this equation: the leader centric elements and the team-centric elements. Dobni and Klassen illustrate this really well in a paper published in the Journal of Innovation, JIM 3, 1 (2015) 104-121, where they document the Drivers of Innovation. The infographic below and reference chart over-page are reference tools to assist you in your future drives for innovation.

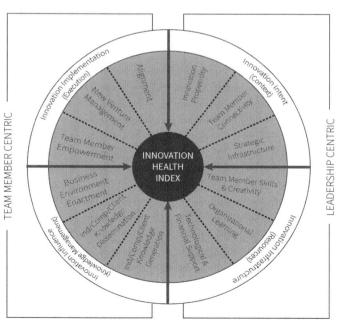

Adapted from Dobni & Klassen's Journal of Innovation Article

DRIVERS OF INNOVATION

① The first quadrant of their model stems from Leadership and is Innovation Intent, or context. Dobni and Klassen describe Innovation Intent factors as:

▶▶ Innovation Propensity: The degree to which the organization has formally established, within their business model, architecture to develop and sustain innovation. This would be communicated through vision, goals, and objectives, and adopted by the senior leadership team.

▶▶ Employee Connectivity: This involves how employees think of themselves vis-à-vis their colleagues. For example, do they feel that they can contribute? Do they feel valued and equitably treated? Do they trust and respect management? Do they resonate with what the organization is doing, and are they working together to achieve the vision?

▶▶ Strategic Infrastructure: Infrastructure for the purposes of innovation involves the business model employed to support the strategy process and innovation overall.

---

② The second quadrant of Dobni and Klassen's model is also leadership centric and is Innovation Infrastructure, or resources. They describe these factors as:

▶▶ Employee Skills and Creativity: The extent to which employees have the skills to be innovative. This includes levels of personal creativity and the surrounding environment (time and space) to allow their skills and creativity to be utilized.

▶▶ Organizational Learning: Properly tooling employees involves committed education and training programs that focus on developing processes that facilitate the learning of new behaviors, and then post training reinforcement.

▶▶ Technical and Financial Support: The extent to which the organization provides resources (financial, time, people, other) to support innovation initiatives.

3 The third quadrant rests on the team side of the 'equation', and that is Innovation Influence, or knowledge management. Dobni and Klassen describe these as:

▶▶ Knowledge Generation: The environment to support knowledge generation by employees from all stakeholders of the company including industry and organizational value chain knowledge.

▶▶ Knowledge Dissemination: The environment to support the dissemination of knowledge to the right people on a timely basis.

▶▶ Business Environment Enactment: The ability of employees, based on knowledge generation and dissemination, to understand the dynamics of their business environment in efforts to define value-added projects and initiatives. These advantages can be identified by observing and understanding the industry, competitors and stakeholders, emerging technology, channels, knowledge flows, and future cluster development.

4 The fourth quadrant demonstrates execution and again rests with the team. This is Innovation Implementation. Dobni and Klassen outline these elements as:

▶▶ Employee Empowerment: This involves the psychological empowerment of employees and their perceived ability/confidence to undertake autonomous actions that contribute to value creation.

▶▶ New Venture Management: This involves the level or degree to which employees can pursue what appear to be opportunities or initiatives with less certainty than they are traditionally comfortable with or for which policies allow for (i.e. entrepreneurial activity).

▶▶ Alignment: This is a measure of alignment to support desired innovation-related behaviors. For example, the performance management and management control systems, and the alignment of innovation strategy with the organization's strategy.

If you go through each of these descriptions and assess your company's culture as it relates to innovation, you will see how much Affinity can underwrite innovation. You will also get a sense of your propensity for innovation as a leader.

In their research, Dobni and Klassen interviewed over 1,100 business leaders from Fortune 1000 companies.

They discovered that breaking the inertia of the status quo was one of the top barriers to innovation and that leaders who communicated a strong need for holistic change and were strategically developing and sustaining innovation were leading their companies to outperform their competition and being rewarded with value creation.

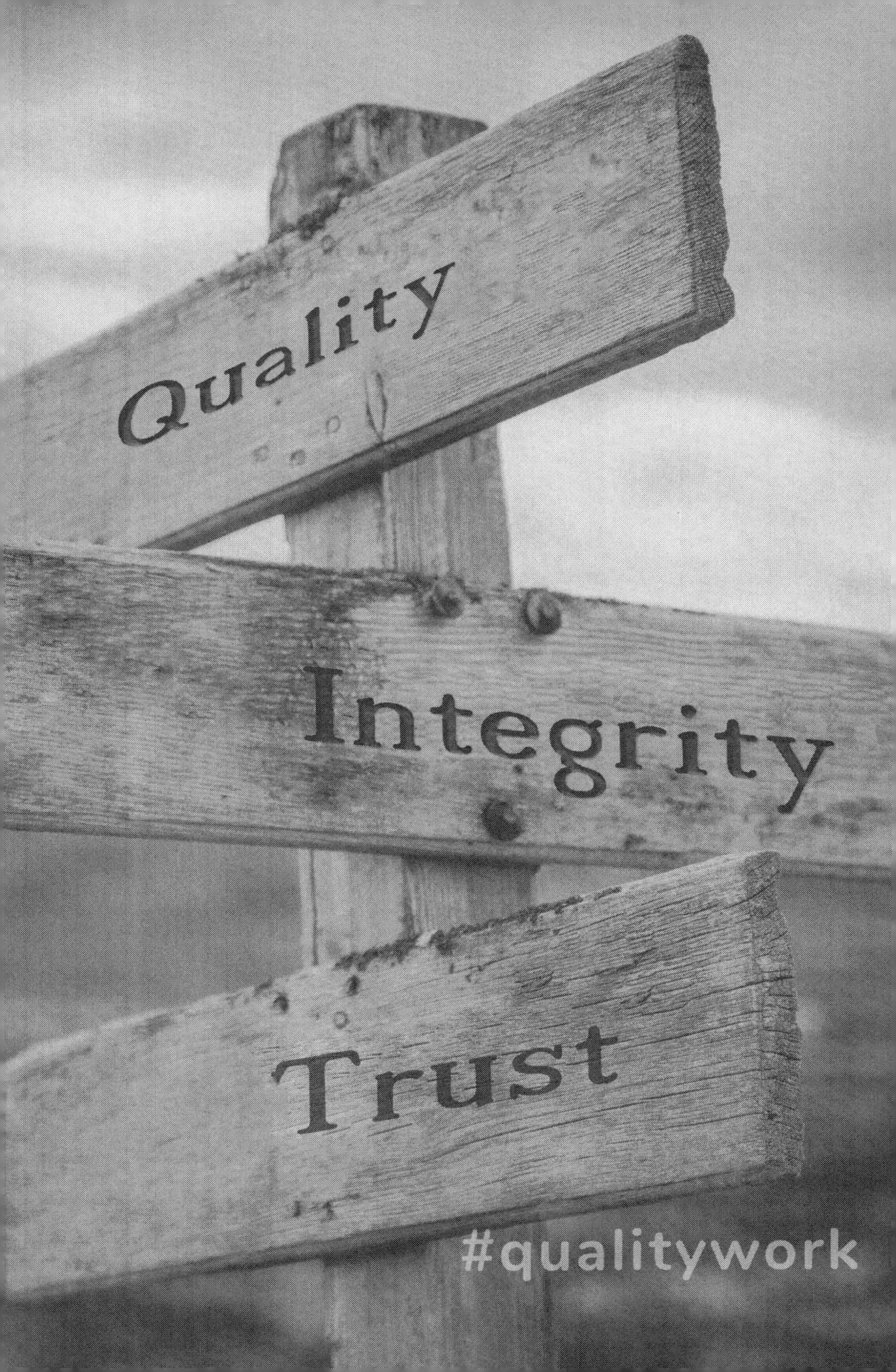
Quality
Integrity
Trust
#qualitywork

CHAPTER 22

Byproduct - Quality Work Happens

by·prod·uct
noun

1. an incidental or secondary product made in the synthesis of something else

When you embed Affinity into your company, quality work becomes a byproduct. In other words, quality work happens.

Creating a consciously positive work environment leads to dramatic decreases in stress, significant increases in team engagement, and increased retention.

When you develop a positive and mindful culture, you will inevitably achieve increased customer satisfaction, higher productivity levels, and a vastly improved financial performance.

Examples of these many benefits abound. In a longitudinal study by the Queen's School of Business where over 110,000 surveys were completed over a ten year period, the studies data showed that companies with the most engaged and aligned employees achieved:**

1. 65% increase in share price
2. 26% lower team member turnover
3. 100% more unsolicited employment applications
4. 20% less absenteeism
5. 15% greater team member productivity
6. up to 30% greater customer satisfaction levels

All this to say that the evidence for creating Affinity is compelling.

The
AFFINITY
FORMULA

GREAT
FINANCIAL RESULTS

AWESOME
CUSTOMER EXPERIENCE

INCREDIBLE
TEAM PERFORMANCE

MINDFUL LEADERSHIP

Intrinsic Benefits of Affinity

As a leader of your organization, the many benefits of creating this conscious culture reflect well on you, reduce your stress, and inevitably improve your career outcomes. If you just reflect back on the six achievements from the Queen's School of Business study, you can see that:

1. **Improved share price** signals that your leadership is moving the company in the right direction. Unlike the Agency-Based model (which puts shareholders first), by threading Affinity through your organization you are creating a Company-Centered model that has as its core tenet the health of the organization and long term returns for shareholders.

2. **Increased team member retention** also reflects well on your leadership as well as the bottom line. Research on the true costs of team member turnover ranges from tens of thousands of dollars, all the way through to 2x their annual salary.** This varies greatly depending on the position, but when you add in all the other intangibles and untracked costs associated with team member turnover, the economic value of retention, over time, is compelling.

3. **Receiving unsolicited applications** can indicate many things, but it often reflects the work culture you have created. In this high mobility era when embarking on your own enterprise is a very real option, you are not just competing for talent with other employers, you are also competing with personal self-realization. To create an environment that attracts talent, you have to weave Affinity through every layer of your organization.

4 <u>Absenteeism</u> reflects many things, and lowered absenteeism will reflect your commitment to the Affinity Principle. The elements of engagement are central to the Affinity Principle where team members have a clear understanding of what's expected of them and have access to the tools and support to get their best work done. Gallup has shown that teams in the top 20% in engagement realize a 41% reduction in absenteeism, and 59% reduction in turnover.

5 <u>Improved productivity</u> is hard to measure or benchmark, but here's a simple statistic from the Society for Human Resource Management:** 58% of employees agree that poor management impedes their productivity. Just the very fact that you're assimilating the contents of this book suggests that you do want to facilitate productivity.

6 <u>The Affinity Formula</u> expounds the direct relationship between the team experience and the customer experience. However, this is a unilateral relationship. In a study by Hoseong Jeong and Beomjoon Choi** on The Relationship Between Employee Satisfaction (ES) and Customer Satisfaction (CS), the researchers demonstrated a very direct positive relationship between Employee Satisfaction and Customer Satisfaction (but little positive relationship between CS and ES). If your team's having a good day, chances are your customers are going to reap the benefits of that positive experience, and much of that will ultimately be a reflection of your leadership.

Quality Work

When we talk about Quality Work as a byproduct of the Affinity Formula, we are really talking about the byproduct of your leadership.

Customer satisfaction and in turn increased profitability can be significantly impacted by creating an improved team members' experience. This begins by hiring talented team members who exhibit the characteristics discussed throughout this book. I've also discussed the need for new team members to complement your existing team. Understanding the components and nuances of your team allows you to better define and hire for the missing elements.

▶▶ *When team members are in the right positions, enjoying the work they do, quality work happens.*

▶▶ *When team members feel good about the people they work with and work for, quality work happens.*

▶▶ *When the financial benefits reflect their productivity and performance, quality work happens.*

▶▶ *When team members have opportunities to grow and improve, quality work happens.*

▶▶ *When team members feel acknowledged and respected, quality work happens.*

Affinity and Happiness

In fact, when the elements of Affinity are aligned, quality work happens and *happiness* in the workplace increases . . . or is it the other way around?

I haven't discussed happiness at length in this book, but it probably sits at the top of most people's personal and professional goals. It also is inherently intertwined in the many layers of Affinity we have discussed herein. According to a study by the University of Warwick, happy team members are 12% more productive than their unhappy counterparts. They are also more likely to enjoy good health and *"smooth flowing"* professional and personal relationships.

Dr. Christine Carter, a senior research associate at the University of California, determined that being happy at work doesn't mean universal acceptance, or the complete absence of negative stress; it is just the power through which we can widen our perspective and bounce back from negativities.

This relates very directly to the Growth Mindset we discussed at length earlier in the book.

Caleb Papineau, from TINYpulse, has demonstrated how workplace happiness improves productivity and creativity. TINYpulse develops software tools to help businesses engage and develop high-performing teams. They have over 1,000 companies they work with including Michelin, Stitch Fix, HubSpot, Deloitte, Capital One, and Brooks Shoes & Apparel. In Papineau's statistical analysis he revealed that:

> ▶▶ *Happy people are 31% more productive and three times more creative than others*
>
> ▶▶ *Happiness can improve business profitability by 147%*
>
> ▶▶ *75% of individuals leave jobs because they are unhappy with the boss rather than the job*

This last point brings back into focus the heart of Affinity and the implicit relationship between your actions and words, and the performance of your company.

Quality work happens when *you*, as a leader:

- ►► Inspire
- ►► Provide Vision
- ►► Demonstrate Administrative Competence
- ►► Encourage Team Integration
- ►► Demonstrate Integrity
- ►► Have a Performance Orientation
- ►► Employ Diplomacy
- ►► Are Decisive

Quality work happens when *team members*:

- ►► Have Clarity of Purpose and Expectations
- ►► Are Raised Up
- ►► Are Encouraged to Unleash Their Gifts
- ►► Know How Much You Care
- ►► Have a Voice
- ►► See the Real You
- ►► Are Well Equipped for Their Work
- ►► Feel Nurtured and Mentored
- ►► Are Encouraged to Grow, Be Curious and Learn
- ►► Know You're Willing to Innovate

#feedbackloops

CHAPTER 23

Loops - Measurement and Feedback: Performance Orientation

loop
noun

1. a structure, series, or process, the end of which is connected to the beginning

When we have a performance orientation, we need to measure and induce feedback in order to determine if performance is improving, stagnating or declining. We need to incorporate feedback loops in this process of refinement.

How we manage this feedback will vary, and typically as leaders we can demonstrate a 'Results Orientation,' or a 'Process Orientation,' depending on the situation and our propensity.

When we have a Results Orientation, we are primarily concerned with the outcome.

A Results Oriented leader can at times adopt a win at any cost attitude and fail to consider the long term consequences or the *debris in their wake*. When we focus exclusively on the results, we can lose some of the nuance in the numbers.

This nuance often translates into the longer term financial impact of our decisions and orientation.

Part of the responsibility of the consummate leader is to look to the horizon while still keeping their eye on where they tread.

Yet there are constant demands in business to have a results based orientation.

The Process-Oriented leader is also concerned with success, but they're also concerned with how that success is achieved. There is an orientation toward performing better today than they did yesterday.

This can be perceived as a more incremental path, or as I would suggest, a more *mindful* path in the right situations.

There are many situations where a process based orientation is preferred in business.

There are also distinct differences between men and women when it comes to these orientations. Ultimately, the orientation you choose depends on the context, and on you.

In two independent studies, researchers found that under stress men and women behave very differently, but maybe not in the way we might typically think. Ruud van den Bos, a neurobiologist at Radboud University in the Netherlands and Mara Mather, a cognitive neuroscientist at the University of Southern California, both determined that when under stress, men become more eager to take risks and women tend to weigh options and look for incremental gains.

As with most things, there are benefits in both responses. Men tend to become Results-Oriented when the pressures on, even if there's only a slim chance of a highly rewarding outcome. Under pressure, men take risks they normally would not, whereas women move into a more Process Orientated approach and look to balance the risks against more incremental rewards. Both bring unique strengths to decision making.

This underwrites the need for diversity in our leadership teams and our decision making processes.

It also speaks to the need to have both; a process orientation and a results orientation when measuring and seeking feedback on Affinity and performance.

Achieving Affinity within your organization is a process and takes time. However, there are short term risks and inevitable challenges to be faced in this metamorphosis.

Stakeholders, including yourself, will rarely be content with the achievement of Nirvana within your organization, without some real and tangible short term performance improvement to underwrite the journey in search of this optimal state.

Gauging Your Business Success Along the Way

More tangible measurements for performance that can help seed and underwrite your efforts include Sales Revenues, Net Profits, Gross Margins, EBITDA, Month-on-Month Performances, and Year-on-Year Comparisons, and so forth.

Important measures can also include things like Cost of Acquisition of Customers, Customer Retention, Customer Loyalty, and Net Promoter Scores®(NPS®).

This last metric, NPS®, has been shown to clearly reflect growth potential in companies. By measuring how well you have achieved customer loyalty you are in turn predicting repeat business. Happy customers tell others about your products or services and referrals and further repeat business ensues.

My point here is that the NPS® metric is a great measure of Affinity and can be measured easily and routinely, providing important insights into your journey toward Affinity in your organization.

NPS NOTE:

Importantly, NPS has a positive correlation to future growth. Fred Reicheld's original data has been substantiated by many independent researchers and organizations and is a reliable predictor of growth in 79% of industries**

Fred Reichheld and Rob Markey have also shown conclusively that in addition to measuring and tracking customer loyalty, you need operational processes to support action and learning by front-line employees. These processes reflect aspects of Affinity of Team. Reicheld and Markey also acknowledge that a sustained commitment from leaders who model inspirational behaviors is fundamental. This is Affinity of Leadership.**

Measuring Affinity of Team

In trying to measure elements of Affinity within your organization, the Gallup Q12 "Employee Engagement Survey" (see q12.gallup.com) provides a 12-question survey that measures team member engagement and highlights strengths and opportunities within your organization to impact performance outcomes.

Gallup has results from over 35 million team members surveyed around the world and as with all measures, benchmarking yourself against others both within and outside your industry is critical. More importantly, measuring team member engagement over time will reflect your efforts to increase engagement and Affinity within your team.

Simpler still, you can ask the Net Promoter Score® (NPS®) question of your team, eNPS® (employeeNPS®), "How likely are you to recommend (insert your company name) to a friend or colleague?"

I would also recommend adding an open-ended question to the eNPS® question. For example, that question could be:

> ▶▶   *"How can we improve your experience on our team?"*
>
> ▶▶   *"What do you like most/least about (insert your company name)?"*
>
> ▶▶   *"What is the one thing we could do to make you happier at (insert your company name)?"*

With regard to measuring happiness, Madhuleena Chowdhury, BA, in a great article, "Happiness at Work: 10 Tips for How to be Happy at Work" on PositivePsychology.com, offers tips and recommendations including recommended surveys and questionnaires to measure this subjective metric. It is worth exploring some of these tools in your quest to understand if happiness is augmenting your quest for Affinity within your organization.

Regardless of the metrics you choose, looping back, and measuring any of these factors consistently over time will help you gauge the value of your efforts from a cultural standpoint.

Measuring Affinity of Leadership

It is also critical to measure the Affinity within your leadership team. I invite you to utilize the Affinity in Leadership Appraisal and other resources that we have developed to assist you. These resources are located at affinityprinciple.com and are constantly revised and updated.

The Affinity in Leadership Appraisal results is best used as a benchmark. Depending on your results, they can help you focus on the areas of opportunity that exist for you in your personal development of Affinity. Revisiting this tool at regular intervals will help you gauge your efforts to increase Affinity in your leadership behaviors.

Mindful Communication of Feedback

Consistent and ongoing feedback is also a critical gauge of less tangible elements of your business. Feedback loops enhance communications.

Importantly feedback should flow in both directions and earlier in the book I highlighted the importance of *listening to your team.*

I suggested that feedback should be threaded through daily and rhythmic activities. Feedback should be given, sought, and received. It can be as simple as real time in person feedback, or it can be a more structured and detailed discussions or scalable mechanisms.

As a leader, feedback to your team members ideally needs to be regular and unsolicited. It also needs to be formalized in more structured feedback discussions.

Importantly, any feedback to team members should be specific.

For example, "I really appreciate how promptly you responded to my request for more information, and the fact that you had that information readily available. Thank you!"

More structured feedback should happen on a rhythmic basis and on an as-needed basis. Rhythmic feedback loops can occur based upon work cycles, such as at the completion of a project, or on a seasonal basis if your company has a normal review process. They can occur on anniversaries as well. One advantage of this anniversary cycle is that it spreads team reviews out over the year.

Earlier on I suggested that position descriptions can be a great instrument to both review a team members' performance, but also to receive feedback.

This is a good example of a feedback mechanism that happens on a rhythmic basis. Reviewing position descriptions should be a scheduled activity and gives you the chance to reflect on the role and the team member.

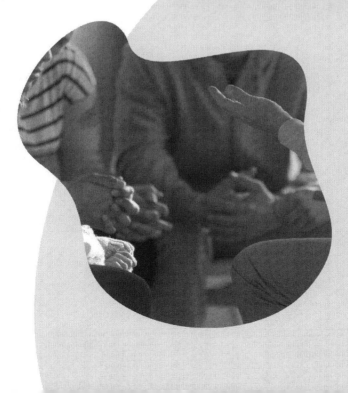

Feedback Tips and Suggestions

Regardless of the rhythms and feedback systems you choose and maintain, some simple guidelines apply:

▶▶ Treat every feedback session as an opportunity to receive feedback, and not just give feedback.

▶▶ Anecdotal feedback should be given in a timely manner, ideally as soon as possible.
  ▶ The disclaimer to this is if you are worked up over what occurred and feel you need some time to settle, give yourself that time . . . maybe sitting on it overnight.
  ▶ In situations where stress is induced, I try to apply the Covey habit of *first seeking to understand and then to be understood.*

▶▶ *Never* give negative feedback in front of other team members.

▶▶ Allow enough time to give AND receive feedback. Don't be rushed, or do it at a time where either of you are likely to be watching the clock.

▶▶ Give feedback in person whenever and wherever possible.
  ▶ In these situations, do not physically position your team member at a disadvantage. Ideally provide the feedback in a situation where it feels you're on equal footing e.g. sitting in the same chairs, at a round table or coffee table, without barriers between you.
  ▶ You should be very present and mindful in these scenarios to receive feedback both verbally and physically, e.g. body language.
    ▶ Be aware of your own body language and what you may be conveying subliminally.

▶▶ Be prepared for the interaction.
  ▶ Find an appropriate location for the discussion.
  ▶ Before launching into the meat of the conversation, break

the ice. For example, ask about the team members day, their family, their interests etc. break the ice, especially in potentially stressful situations.

▶ Be specific in your feedback and have specific questions to solicit feedback.

▶▶ If you are seeking change or improvement from the team member, discuss your expectations and clearly distill any consensus of understanding you achieve in the feedback session.

▶▶ If things unravel in the discussion, be prepared to take a time out and reschedule for a later time.

▶▶ After the discussion, be conscious of what is confidential and what can and needs to be shared with the appropriate people on your team.

▶▶ Depending on the nature of the feedback session, it may make sense to document the content of the discussion and the outcomes agreed upon.

▶ In the case of formal feedback sessions, it is usual for the team member to receive a copy of your feedback that you are placing in their file.

Feedback Upward

As leaders, we have often given and received a great deal of feedback during our careers. As a result, we may be more skilled at the art of giving constructive feedback and receiving feedback than our team members. However, there are always opportunities to improve our skills in this important area. Equally, we should equip our team members to be able to receive feedback AND provide feedback upwards.

Team members that report to you will always feel at somewhat of a disadvantage in any feedback exchange, so building trust and equipping them to provide constructive feedback is essential.

Your openness to feedback and your ability to create trust from team members will determine the quality and quantity of feedback you receive. When I say quality, I mean whether or not you are receiving truth.

Are your team members willing to give you feedback they think you may not want to hear?

TIP: You set the tone for this in everything you say and do and even more importantly, in the reactions you have to feedback over time.

When equipping your team to provide feedback, formal training can be incredibly beneficial. Importantly, this training should teach the art of providing constructive feedback, including:

▶▶ The team member's understanding of their intrinsic motivation for providing feedback, e.g. they want something to be changed, or they want you to be aware of something, or they just need you to listen.

> ▶ It helps if the team member can announce their motivation up front in the discussion.

▶▶ How to present the feedback in a positive way, that it is both honest AND likely to be received in the right way.

▶▶ Ensure that any feedback is specific and clear. Generalizations won't help the leader understand what needs to change, or what the exact problem is, e.g. "I don't think my supervisor likes me." This is OK as an introduction, but needs to be underwritten by specific examples that can be corroborated.

▶▶ Acknowledging any good things that are happening, or steps that have been made in the right direction.

▶▶ The team member should look for feedback and ascertain if their points are being accepted or rejected. They should also try and determine what actions are intended on the basis of the feedback.

Coaching team members on providing timely and constructive feedback to subordinates, their peers, and to their leaders, is also a critical step in enhancing communications throughout your organization. It is a significant step in the pursuit of Affinity. It should also be backed up by formal systems to allow for feedback to flow upwards easily.

Providing access to feedback systems is one way to encourage upward feedback. These can range from polling systems and engagement tools to pulse surveys and anonymous feedback mechanisms. These systems can be available year-round, distributed routinely, or seasonally. They can also be administered in situations where you need specific feedback on a specific topic but should be handled judiciously.

Feedback is an essential communication tool within a healthy organization and when it flows freely and easily up and down the organization, Affinity will also flow.

Measurement and Improvement

The old adage, "You can't manage what you don't measure," was credited to W. Edwards Deming who helped launch the Total Quality Management (TQM) movement.

Peter Drucker, who has written almost 40 books on management and is known as one of the foremost thinkers in business management in the 20th century, upgraded this statement by saying:**

"If you can't measure it, you can't improve it."

I see Drucker's version as a preferred way to think about measuring and seeking feedback because as managers and leaders we should seek to improve and not just manage.

In seeking to improve the performance of our people and our organization, we constantly need to measure and gather data points. We look for trends and opportunities to guide us. That guidance ideally helps us extend our lead in highly competitive markets and times. We need to look for beacons in the distance, and rocks that appear almost without warning at our bow.

We need feedback and measurements to be taken constantly and consistently. We need to measure all those things we seek to manage in order to exact positive change in our organizations. This change management is leveraged through Affinity within your team.

#peoplefirstalways

CONCLUSION

If we seek to create Affinity within our organizations, we need to be present and focus our energy and intent in order to consciously improve our team's experience and performance. In turn, our customers will reap the rewards. The upside of this improved customer experience is improved financial outcomes.

The
**AFFINITY
FORMULA**

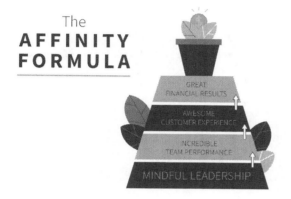

As I have suggested throughout this book, you are the catalyst to initiate this momentum and create a continuum.

Peter Drucker's other equally famous quote highlights the common thread that I feel creates true alignment with Affinity:

"Management is doing things right; leadership is doing the right things."

Management is doing things, often many things, the right way!
Leadership is doing the necessary things, for the right reasons!

When who you are and what you represent is aligned with your core values and intrinsic purpose, your team will follow you with the certainty that cements this foundation of trust . . .

and Affinity follows.

#gratitude

ACKNOWLEDGMENTS

I feel as if I have led a charmed life. I have had the benefit of some amazing opportunities as well as my share of challenges over my career. All these experiences have helped shape and define my leadership style and how I live my life today.

In truth, no one thing has been more fundamental in shaping my life today than my family.

My wife Jana has been my partner and advocate in life and in business. Jana is the mother of our two amazing children, Jack and Ellie. She has amassed an amazing body of work as a Designer, Creative Director, and Artist. Her contributions to this book speak for themselves. Jana brought this book to life in ways I could only have imagined.

Jana also drops truth bombs on me routinely and has truly inspired me to do my best work, without compromise. In turn, she has orchestrated all my branding, marketing, web, and social content and distribution. It is impossible to fully describe my appreciation for these mammoth and ongoing contributions.

I would also like to thank Wistar Murray for providing an incredibly valuable, insightful, and heartening editorial overview of the book. Thank you!

My heartfelt thanks to Tim Rhode. Tim is a longtime friend, colleague, and advocate, who dug deep into an early draft of this book to give me both granular and functional feedback that added immense value. Your constant friendship and positive can-do attitude are so appreciated.

I also want to thank the mentors that have shared so much with me over the years. Especially Phil Wendel, whose sage advice was always valued.

Most of all, I want to thank the many team members that I have worked with over the years. They have taught me invaluable lessons that have helped me define and refine the Affinity concept, formula, and principle. My appreciation knows no bounds.

PHOTO ON LEFT: Thanks also to Phoebe for providing regular screen breaks with her need to get out of the office and go chase squirrels.

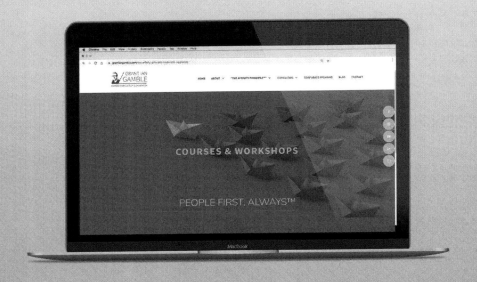

#learn

COURSES & WORKSHOPS

I offer a growing library of online courses and workshops. You can find a few descriptions of my courses and workshops on the following pages. To see our full list of offerings, please visit https://grantiangamble.com/courses-workshops/ or scan the QR code with your phone.

Courses or Quests

THE CENTERED LEADER - ACHIEVING AFFINITY OF SELF

The core tenet of this program is centeredness or mindfulness.

Bain and Co. determined that out of 33 traits that inspired colleagues, centeredness is the most important inspirational quality a leader can exhibit. This program will focus on what it takes to achieve and maintain this balanced and conscious state.

In pursuit of centeredness, we will explore 8 fundamentals that are covered in my book, "The Affinity Principle." These fundamentals were distilled from the GLOBE 2020 CEO Study. This massive research project gathered data and feedback from 1,000 CEO's and over 5,000 senior executives from a variety of industries across 24 countries. The study determined these 8 primary CEO leadership behaviors most impacted Top Management Team Dedication and Firms Competitive Performance.

This program will cover these behaviors and how you might leverage or enhance those behaviors in you.

UNLOCK YOUR INTRINSIC POTENTIAL - YOUR KEY TO SUCCESS

In this program, we focus on awakening your Intrinsic Potential (you can also think of it as your "Intellectual Property," or "IP"). Each of us has innate talents and abilities. Often, these gifts are suppressed in our formative years by external expectations and imprints that steer us in a direction we may not be best suited for. Parenting and schooling have a tremendous impact on how these aspects of our true selves are either expanded or contracted.

More often than not, due to societal pressures and the schooling system, which is built around the lowest common denominator, our intrinsic talents and abilities get lost in the system.

This program looks at the imprints that have formed over the course of our lives and we explore ways to unlock and leverage your true potential into the success you desire.

Fundamental to this program is seeing into one's true nature, or "Kenshō". This is a Zen Buddhist term; Ken means "seeing," shō means "nature," or "essence". The term for this awakening through comprehension and understanding of the self is "Satori."

As you begin focusing on your "true nature," you will begin to expand and unleash your intrinsic gifts. We will create this momentum through exploring and developing 8 key elements:

1. MIND
2. BODY
3. SOUL
4. WORK
5. LOVE
6. REST
7. FUEL
8. PLAY

Each of these facets of your life will help you bring clarity and focus to your intrinsic potential, and allow you to expand that potential exponentially.

Mini Courses

MAKING MEETINGS MATTER

The cost of poorly organized meetings in 2019 almost topped $400 Billion in the US alone (Doodle's 2019 State of Meetings Report).

WHY?

- 92% of attendees self report that they work on other things during meetings
- Only 37% of meetings work to an agenda
- 57% of people multitask on a phone call (only 4% of people multitask on a video call)
- Irrelevant attendees slow progress in meetings by 31%
- 65% of senior managers said meetings reduce their ability to complete their own work

THE SOLUTION

There is no single solution but for example simply using an agenda can reduce meeting time up to 80%.

THIS 3-PART COURSE INCLUDES:

PART 1: The Basics: 4 Key Areas of Focus When Considering Refining Your Internal Meeting Performance

PART 2: Ways You Can Be a Mindful Meeting Steward as the Leader or Man ager

PART 3: The Stand-Up: One Of the Most Effective Meet ing Formats

INCREASE YOUR PRODUCTIVITY: GAIN TRACTION AMID ENDLESS DISTRACTIONS

PROBLEM

Researchers have proven that when switching between tasks comprehension decreases and the speed of completion is decreased by up to 40%. They've also shown a reduction in the efficiency in completing tasks of up to 4x.

Put simply, learning is seriously impaired when you're multitasking, and errors increase when we're dividing our attention between two or more tasks.

THE SOLUTION

Single-tasking actually amplifies comprehension, improves completion of task efficiency, and reduces errors.

THIS 3-PART COURSE INCLUDES:

PART 1: Exploring the price we pay when we multitask

PART 2: Expanding and solidifying the benefits of single-tasking

PART 3: Simple tips and tools to effectively shift from multitasking to single-tasking

Through this mini-course, you can experience the immense benefits of being present and engaged in one activity at a time. Using this powerful technique will enhance your memory, decrease your stress levels, enhance your creativity, and improve your efficiency and productivity.

RESOURCES, REFERENCES, AND READING

Affinity Principle™ Leadership Appraisal

This tool is based on the Globe 2020 Report of CEO Leadership Behaviors and Effectiveness. It reviews the primary leadership categories that most influence top management teams' dedication and overall company performance. To take the Leadership Appraisal, visit the URL below or scan the QR code with the camera on your phone.

https://grantiangamble.com/leadership-appraisal-sign-up-form/

Affinity Principle™ Change Management Appraisal

To take the Change Management Appraisal, visit the URL below or scan the QR code with the camera on your phone.

https://grantiangamble.com/change-management-appraisal-sign-up-form/

Affinity Principle™ Inspirational Leadership Review

This Review is based on the Bain Inspirational Leadership Model (see page 46) and can help you highlight your inspirational leadership strengths and provide focus for continued growth in your leadership style and effectiveness. To take the Inspirational Leadership Review, visit the URL below or scan the QR code with the camera on your phone.

https://grantiangamble.com/inspirational-leadership-review-sign-up-form/

Affinity Principle™ Leadership & Management Discovery

This inventory helps you understand your current team's strengths and define areas where they may need support and/or development.

https://grantiangamble.com/leadership-and-management-discovery-sign-up/

Arthur D.Little - ADL is a management consulting firm focused on strategy, innovation, and transformation. They conduct the Global Innovation Excellence Survey which helps companies benchmark their innovation performance against peers and understand the opportunities to improve their innovation

practices,
https://www.adlittle.com/en/insights/viewpoints/arthur-d-little's-global-inno-vation-excellence-survey

Bain and Company, Inc. - Bain & Company is an elite management consulting firm serving a global clientele. Mark Horwitch and Meredith Whipple Callahan are senior team members at Bain and identified 33 distinct and tangible attributes that are statistically significant in creating inspiration in others.
https://www.bain.com/insights/how-leaders-inspire-cracking-the-code/

"Blue Ocean Strategy," by W. Chan Kim, Renée Mauborgne - Blue Ocean Strategy is the simultaneous pursuit of differentiation and low cost to open up a new market space and create new demand. It is about creating and capturing uncontested market space, thereby making the competition irrelevant.
https://www.blueoceanstrategy.com/what-is-blue-ocean-strategy/

Brené Brown - is an author and researcher who has spent the last two decades studying courage, vulnerability, shame, and empathy. Brown argues that vulnerability and authenticity are at the root of all human connections.
https://brenebrown.com

C. Brooke Dobni and Mark Klaasen - Dobni and Klaasen have conducted an enormous amount of groundbreaking research on innovation. The Global State of Innovation Survey assesses the cultures of innovation and innovation practices across 11 countries, pinpointing contemporary practices in innovation and the areas in which organizations are succeeding and struggling.
http://innovationone.io/research/

Cohen Center for the Humanities - The Cohen Center at James Madison University fosters intellectual engagement, interdisciplinary collaboration, and inquiry while creating a community for students and faculty.
https://www.jmu.edu/cohencenter/

Daniel Goleman - Daniel has written several books on Emotional Intelligence where Goleman posits that emotional intelligence is as important as IQ for success in academic, professional, social, and interpersonal aspects of one's life.
http://www.danielgoleman.info

"Death by Meetings", by Patrick Lencioni - Lencioni's business fable takes on meetings - why we hate them, why we shouldn't, and how to make them great. Lencioni also wrote, "The Five Dysfunctions of a Team" which is also an evergreen.
https://www.tablegroup.com

"Flow: The Psychology of Happiness," Mihaly Csikszentmihalyi describes the optimal state where we encounter a challenge that is testing for our skills, and yet our skills and capacities are such that it is possible to meet this challenge. He is the 'father' of Flow.
https://flowleadership.org

Francesca Gino, is an author and professor at Harvard Business School. Gino studies how people can have more productive, creative, and fulfilling lives.
https://francescagino.com

Frances Frei's Triangle of Trust - Frei is a best selling author and faculty at Harvard Business School. The Triangle of Trust framework delivers a crash course on stakeholder trust: how to build it, maintain it, and restore it when lost.
https://www.hbs.edu/faculty/Pages/profile.aspx?facId=6587

Gallup Engagement - Gallup has a simple, but powerful, tool for measuring team member (employee) engagement. They also have vast resources to help go beyond the measurement of engagement. Gallup's work is a central reference point for this text.
https://www.gallup.com/workplace/229424/employee-engagement.aspx

Globe 2020 CEO Study - This massive study provides convincing evidence as to which leadership behaviors are likely to be most successful and which should be avoided and is a central reference point for this text.
https://globeproject.com/study_2014

Ichak Adizes - The Adizes Management Style Indicator and Organizational Lifecycles model helps team members work more effectively together. It also helps organizations, as they grow, to predict organizational patterns of behavior, and these insights help that organization rise to the next level.
https://adizes.com

"In Search of Excellence," by Tom Peters and Robert Waterman Jr. - Profiling 43 companies, In Search of Excellence describes 8 basic principles that made these organizations successful. Although dated this best-selling book has been a must-read for management teams for decades.
https://tompeters.com/writing/books/

John Maxwell - John C. Maxwell is an American author and speaker who has written many books on leadership, two of which are referenced in this text, "How Successful People Lead" and "21 Irrefutable Laws of Leadership."
https://www.johnmaxwell.com

Jonathan Cohen - In his work at Princeton, Cohen researches the neurobiological mechanisms underlying cognitive control. Cognitive control is the ability to guide attention, thought, and action in accordance with goals or intentions.
https://pni.princeton.edu/faculty/jonathan-cohen

Kim Cameron - Cameron is a researcher at the University of Michigan who became interested in organizations that were downsizing and the impact on the organization. His research honed in on companies that were characterized by virtuous practices—for example, forgiveness, compassion, integrity, trust, optimism, kindness—and how they tended to avoid the declining performance associated with downsizing
https://positiveorgs.bus.umich.edu/people/kim-s-cameron/

"Lead with Humility" by Jeffrey A. Krames - Pope Frances's ability to inspire the world is unprecedented in modern times. "Lead with Humility" reveals the power of his methods, and give guidance for anyone to lead with humility.
https://www.goodreads.com/en/book/show/22238514-lead-with-humility

"Meetings Suck", by Cameron Herrold - Herrold actually contends that meetings don't suck; we suck at running meetings. When done right, meetings not only work, they make people and companies better.
https://cameronherold.com

Myers-Briggs Type Indicator® (MBTI®) was developed by Isabel Briggs Myers, and Katharine Briggs - In developing the Myers-Briggs Type Indicator [instrument] Myers and Briggs made the insights of type theory accessible to individuals and groups.
https://www.myersbriggs.org/my-mbti-personality-type/mbti-basics/

Net Promoter®, Net Promoter Score®, and NPS® are trademarks of Satmetrix Systems, Inc., Bain & Company, Inc., and Fred Reichheld. Net Promoter Score®, or NPS®, measures customer experience and predicts business growth. This proven metric provides a core measurement for customer experience management programs worldwide.
https://www.netpromoter.com/know/

Queen's Centre for Business Venturing (QCBV) - The Centre for Business Venturing at Smith School of Business is a leading and source of knowledge and expertise in the creation, leadership, and management of new ventures.
https://smith.queensu.ca/centres/business-venturing/index.php

"The Art of War," by Sun Tzu - Dating back to 500B.C. this text has morphed from military circles into the business world. Its tenets have been transposed into modern business management principles.   h t t p s : //www.goodreads.com/book/show/42268647-the-art-of-war-with-study-guide?from_search=true&from_srp=true&qid=zCVPxePp4T&rank=4

TINYpulse - TINYpulse is a feedback-based tool that encourages teams to provide input. They provide leaders with quantitative feedback with the goal to help create a superior workplace culture and a happier team. https://www.tinypulse.com

Made in the USA
Monee, IL
25 August 2020